"First, I wish every book was written as simply and yet profoundly as this book. It makes reading a pleasure with understanding being the goal. Second… I liked it! I felt as though he gave me something to build my Christian Walk stronger with. Thank you Mike for a great read!"

—Leo Giovinetti
Pastor Mission Valley Christian Fellowship
"Real Life Radio"

"Mike Lutz's new book, *Discovering God's Will for Your Life: Your Journey with God,* has an exciting and fresh approach to *discovering* God's will. It does not contain any tired chapters titles. With chapter like "You Talkin' to Me?" and "I Object!" who could go wrong?"

— Lenya Heitzig
Bible Teacher, Author

"If you are looking for practical information relating to God's will for your life, this is the book for you. I recommend this book to anyone seeking to honor God's will with their lives. I served on staff at a church with Mike Lutz and love his heart for the Lord, I believe you will be blessed by his writing."

— Levi Lusko
Pastor, Fresh Life Church

"Mike Lutz's book is an excellent, encouraging, and informative book that will certainly be a blessing to any and all who read it. I enjoy Mike's writing style, and his insights and encouragements concerning the basic elements of our faith that ultimately lead to maturity are spot on! May you be blessed as you read, and may you put into practice what you are learning!"

— David Rosales
Pastor Calvary Chapel Chino Valley, CA
"A Sure Foundation Radio"

DISCOVERING
GOD'S WILL
FOR YOUR LIFE

Your journey **with God**

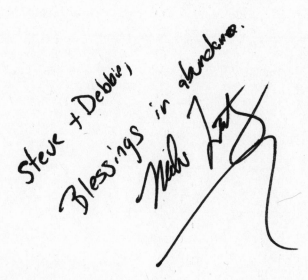

Steve + Debbie,
Blessings in abundance.

DISCOVERING
GOD'S WILL
FOR YOUR LIFE

Your journey **with God**

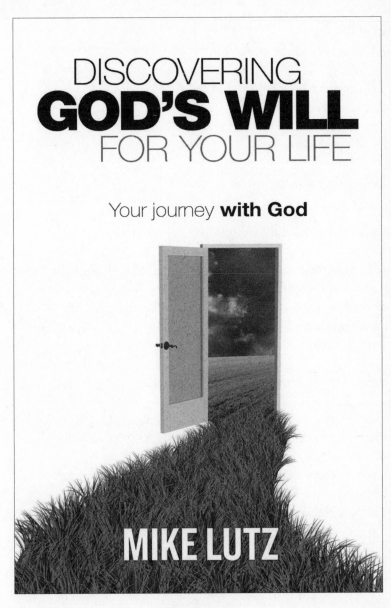

MIKE LUTZ

BRIDGE
LOGOS
FOUNDATION

Alachua, Florida 32615

Bridge-Logos
Alachua, FL 32615 USA

Discovering God's Will for Your Life:
Your Journey with God

by Michael Lutz

Edited by Karla Pedrow

Printed in the United States of America.

Library of Congress Catalog Card Number: 2012940607
International Standard Book Number: 978-0-88270-831-7

DEDICATION

❦

May this book bring glory,

honor,

and praise

to God the Father

and our Lord Jesus Christ.

"My supremest will shall be not to will anything except Thy will, and if I do will it I repent of so willing, and discard the evil will and the undesirable desire."[1]
—C. H. Spurgeon

CONTENTS

൸

Part 3: Where the Rubber Meets the Road

ACKNOWLEDGEMENTS

I would like to give a special thanks to my wife Colette. If it were not for her support, I would not have been able to write this book. Thank you, and I love you.

INTRODUCTION

The Fundamentals

❧

All Scripture is inspired by God and is useful to teach us what is true and to make us realize what is wrong in our lives. It corrects us when we are wrong and teaches us to do what is right. God uses it to prepare and equip his people to do every good work. 2 Timothy 3:16-17, NLT

Do you want to know God's plan for your life? Would you like to know what God wants you to do in a specific situation? How can you use the Bible to help you navigate through this life? The answer begins with the fundamentals.

For several years, I was an assistant golf professional and gave private lessons. Through that experience, I found that people who came for golf lessons all did so for the same reason. It didn't matter whether they had twenty years' experience or whether it was their first time ever to hold a golf club. They all wanted the same thing: to hit the ball straight.

For some, the problem was they were pushing the ball to the right. Others were pulling the ball to the left, while others were popping it straight up. Still others never even made contact with the golf ball. Have you ever felt like that as you try to follow God? You feel pushed and pulled in every direction, and it is as though you are trying to hit a golf ball blindfolded—you are never able to make contact with God.

In golf, a straight shot is the hardest one to consistently achieve. As a teacher, I found the best thing to do, regardless of the golfer's ability, was to always start with the fundamentals. I would often say, "Okay, let's go back to basics." Then I would look to see how they were setting up to the ball, how they were holding the club, or how their stance looked. And the list went on.

In virtually every case, the golfer's problem could be traced back to a difficulty with one of the fundamentals. Even if the golfer was just slightly off in one of the fundamentals, the outcome could be hazardous. Before someone can call himself or herself a golfer, the fundamental principles not only must be understood but also practiced before moving on to the more advanced principles.

What is true for the golfer is also true for the Christian: we must go back to the basics to make certain they are understood and put into practice. This way, we can walk the straight path God has for us. Because much like hitting a straight ball in the game of golf, walking the straight line of faith is the hardest thing to consistently achieve.

The Apostle Paul recognized the importance of starting with the basics when he wrote to the Corinthians, *"I fed you with milk and not with solid food; for until now you were not able to receive it . . ."* (1 Corinthians 3:2).

As we look to God's Word, we will seek to follow God, to see how He relates to us, how He directs us, speaks to us, and leads us. There are many places we can go in the Bible to see how God leads His people, but I chose some of my favorite Scripture passages and some of my favorite people to demonstrate how the fundamentals look in action.

We will take some time looking at the life of Joseph from the Old Testament. In this personal favorite, we will see how God works in and through the life of this faithful young man. In the highest of highs and in the lowest of lows, God never stops working. Also, we will look at the life of Moses and see how God moves in and through the strengths and weaknesses of Moses to accomplish His perfect plan and purpose. Finally, we will seek to understand some fundamentals of how the Bible and God's Holy Spirit work together to guide and direct us. As a result, we will be better prepared to hear Him when He speaks to us, enabling us to be in the best position to follow where He is leading.

In the chapter that follows, we will take a look at the first and most important fundamental for knowing God's will for your life—knowing God himself. As you join me in this journey, you will discover God is our guide, and He has provided us with all the directions and maps we need in order to walk in accordance with His will. *Your Journey With God* will take us to the heart of the issue by highlighting what God has said about following Him. We will take a deep biblical look at how God reveals His will to His people, while at the same time presenting a very practical approach to how this relates to our lives today.

PART ONE

✑

Joseph's Journey of Faith

1

Every Journey
BEGINS
Somewhere

✑

This Book of the Law shall not depart from your mouth, but you shall meditate in it day and night, that you may observe to do according to all that is written in it. For then you will make your way prosperous, and then you will have good success. Joshua 1:8

In order to know God's will, you must first know God. If it is your heart's desire to follow God's plan for your life, and if you want to walk the path God has for you, then you can't take the first step toward knowing God's will unless you first understand what it means to have a personal relationship with Jesus Christ. Following God means knowing Him, and to know Him means that we must first know His Son, Jesus Christ.

God's primary will for you and me can be found in 2 Peter 3:9: *"The Lord is . . . not willing that any should perish but that all should come to repentance."*

God is not off in a distant galaxy, unreachable, unavailable, and uninterested in our lives. He is personally and intimately interested in us—so much so that He sent His only Son Jesus to make a relationship with Him possible: a personal, life-changing, and intimate relationship with God. It is not about religion; it is all about a relationship. It is not about church; it is about Christ. It is not about what you can do for God; it is about what God has *already* done for you.

Jesus, who was fully man and fully God, opened the door for that relationship by paying the price for our sins. This is where your journey begins in a relationship with Jesus and a life lived for Him. To know Jesus Christ personally will change who you are, what you do, why you do it, and how you live your life. If you have ever met a person who claims to be a Christian but hasn't been changed as a result of his or her relationship with Jesus, then you haven't met a true Christian.

If you want to be sure of your salvation, or if you don't think you are saved, or if you simply *hope* you are going to Heaven, then I have good news for you: you *can* know. Salvation isn't a matter of opinion; it is something we can be certain of. If you are reading this book and don't know God, my heart's desire is it will help you to know Him and to follow Him. Allow me to take you through this process in the Conclusion at the back of this book, entitled "How to Know God."

The joy of knowing God is inexpressible, the love of God is limitless, and the peace of God is beyond understanding.

In the lifelong journey of knowing Him, it is my hope that this book will help you learn to follow Him, will help you see how He works, and will teach you to hear that *still, small voice* with which He so often speaks to us.

—

The Next Step

Now, if you are going to have any chance of hearing God, following after Him, and learning His will and His ways, then this next fundamental must become a regular part of your life. It is a daily quiet time with God.

This essential practice is something many believers already know should be a regular part of their daily life, but sadly, many do not consistently make the time for it. I wish this were not the case, but unfortunately, it is a pattern I have seen in counseling session after counseling session and in conversation after conversation. It usually goes something like this:

"Yes, I know I haven't been praying or spending time in God's Word, but. . . ."

Excuses, excuses. How we love to make excuses, no matter how busy our lives are.

Believe me, I know many people are juggling kids, work demands, family and school responsibilities, not to mention health issues you or someone close to you may be facing. But the bottom line is the reasons people give for not having a regular quiet time are nothing more than excuses. You may be saying, "But Mike, you just don't understand my situation."

Honestly, I don't have to. You have the time. Yes, it may require sacrifice, rearranging your schedule, and changing your priorities. Something may need to be taken off your plate, or you may have to scratch something off your to-do list. If you feel that it is totally impossible, then it may take a little extra effort, a little more creativity, or simply a little more diligence to fit it into your already full schedule. And let me just say if your schedule is too full for God, then something needs to go.

It isn't my purpose here to delve into time management skills, but I will say you need to make the time to spend time with God. That is why it is a fundamental, and fundamentals are the building blocks of life. This is your spiritual life, and you can't move forward without it. No more excuses. Be determined to make a fresh start today and then just do it.

If a regular meeting time with God is missing in your life, then everything else you read in this book will be meaningless. There are times in life when circumstances beyond your control will force you to interrupt your normal routine with God and may cause some inconsistencies for a few days. But even during these times, you should still do all you can to stay connected with Him. Maybe you will have a little shorter time with God for a few days. Or maybe you will have to change your time or use different methods, such as listening to audio Bible readings or carrying a few podcast sermons with you to help in a pinch. The exceptions are never to become the rule. Regular, quality quiet time is non-negotiable. Make it your aim never to be out of your regular routine for more than a couple of days, and only when absolutely necessary.

Now that we are clear on the importance and frequency of a quiet time, let's go over what is involved in a quiet time.

First, this is time between you and God alone—no distractions. When possible, seek out a time and place where no one else will be around. It should be a place where you give God your complete and undivided attention. This is a must. Have you ever had one of those conversations where there was too much noise or too many people around? It became hard to hear the person you were speaking with because of all the noise. Maybe it was so distracting that it was hard to hear yourself think. What did you do? You probably sought out a quieter location so you could continue your conversation.

It is the same when it comes to spending time with God. If you have distractions, it is hard to hear God speak. And if your environment is filled with noise, then it can be hard to stay focused. Whether you sit, stand, or go for a walk, it doesn't matter. You can be inside in a comfy chair or at your desk, you can be on your computer, or you can be outside under a tree.

Position and location do not matter. What is important is that your surroundings are not a distraction and do not detract from giving God your full attention. *Quiet* is essential in the quiet time.

Quiet goes a long way in the next aspect of our time with God, which is communication. In any relationship, communication is important because it is the mode by which we share ideas, information, and emotions. Without communication, relationships are destined for difficulties, headed for misunderstandings, filled with frequent frustrations, and, in the worst of cases, they can even face failure.

Your relationship with God is no different, and communication is of the utmost importance. If you do not spend time communicating with God through prayer and allowing God to communicate with you by reading the Bible and letting His Holy Spirit speak to your heart, then that relationship will be destined for difficulties, headed for misunderstandings, filled with frustrations, and in some cases, will face the risk of failure. There is no other single area that is more directly related to a person's ability to know God's will than through their personal time with Him. Neglect it, and you are flying blind. Nurture it, and the world is at your feet, with God lighting the way.

The daily quiet time with God is not only vital in following Him and discovering His will in your life, but it is also critical to your daily spiritual health and well-being. You wouldn't go a day without eating food or drinking water, because your body needs that energy supply to accomplish all the activities of the day. In the same way, we need the spiritual food and water God has made available to us in His Word. It is designed to sustain us and energize us to accomplish all the godly activities we have before us.

There are many challenges we face in life that can be avoided if we remain consistently close to God. It doesn't mean we will be free from difficulty or trials, but it does mean there are many situations we face that could have been avoided if we were spending that quality time with God.

Just like the physical body needs a well-balanced diet to function at peak performance, so does the child of God need a balanced diet of God's Word and prayer. These are essential for us to operate at peak spiritual performance. It is no coincidence that the less time we spend with God, the more difficult life becomes.

Being consistently in communion with God doesn't mean the storms of life won't come crashing in all around us. Actually, God's Word tells us to expect even more storms as Christians, because we are living lives completely contrary to the way the world lives. We are swimming upstream, while everyone else is allowing the current of popular culture to carry them downstream. Jesus told His followers, *"In the world you will have tribulation . . ."* (John 16:33). Peter reminded his readers not to think it strange when trials come (see 1 Peter 4:12-17).

Let me illustrate it this way. What if someone, with great generosity, gave you a big, forty-foot sailboat as a gift, took you out on the ocean, and said, "Okay, go for it! It's all yours!"

There is only one problem: you have never sailed before. Even if it was a calm day out on the water, you still would have trouble knowing what to do, how to navigate, how to trim the sails, how to chart a course, when and where to drop anchor, and the list goes on. Now imagine if the wind began to pick up and the waves came crashing over the side of the boat. You would be in big trouble, wouldn't you?

Now let's take the same gift and imagine that before you received it, you spent every day for three years on that forty-foot boat being taught by an expert. You were shown every square inch of the boat. You learned how to trim the sails, how to navigate in a headwind, how to chart a course, and more. Now with that kind of training, when the winds begin to blow and the waves begin to crash, you will be ready. You will be thoroughly equipped and able to navigate through the storm. Yes, you will get wet and maybe even tossed around a little, but you will be able to navigate through the bad weather and make it safely to shore.

Your daily time with God is time with the Master. He is the expert on life and He trains us and shows us how to chart a course through life's storms. He will show us how to get safely to our destination. There *will be* storms. Things will get difficult, you will get wet, and rest assured, you even will get a little bruised and battered in the process. But with God's Word, you can navigate life's roughest seas, knowing He will lead you to safe harbor.

Allow me to show you a few places in Scripture that illustrate the value of having a daily quiet time with God. Joshua is one of my favorite men of the Bible, and from the beginning to the end of the book that bears his name, we see a man in love with God and His holy Word. God gave Joshua some good advice, which serves as a recipe for success. Its key ingredient: time in God's Word:

This Book of the Law shall not depart from your mouth, but you shall meditate in it day and night, that you may observe to do according to all that is written in it. For then you will make your way prosperous, and then you will have good success. Have I not commanded you? Be strong and of good courage; do not be afraid, nor be dismayed, for the Lord your God is with you wherever you go. (Joshua 1:8-9)

What a promise! What encouragement! But notice the parameters: consistent and continual commitment to God's Word. The promise is dependent upon our proximity to God's Word and the priority we give it. Daily with God—that is the key. Notice in these verses God will give us strength to face whatever life throws at us, because He promises the power of His presence.

The promises of God and the presence of God are two of the greatest forces available to you and me. To have God's presence with us wherever we go is absolutely amazing and mind-blowing. Even though we cannot see God, He is with us and gives us His presence to help us. That is why one of the names for the Holy

Spirit in the New Testament is *Helper*. His presence is our great help.

We must also meditate on God's Word. The word *meditate* means to chew on something over and over again, much like a cow chews its cud. We are to "chew on" Scripture day and night. This will give us a knowledge and understanding of God's Word, which leads us into knowledge and understanding of God. And the more we know and understand God, the more we will be able to observe all that He has commanded us, which leads us to the center of His will. Getting to know God means getting to know His will.

Another key for our daily quiet time with God can be found in a different Joshua, the Joshua of the New Testament. *Yeshua* is the Hebrew name for Joshua, which is also the name *Jesus* (the Greek version of Joshua) in the New Testament. Who better than Jesus to give us a key insight to our daily quiet times with God?

Jesus was a man of prayer. Spend even the shortest amount of time in the gospels and you will come face to face with the priority Jesus gave to prayer. Prayer was so essential to Jesus that He often would pass up food and sleep just to have more time with God, the Father:

"So He Himself often withdrew into the wilderness and prayed." Luke 5:16

"And when He had sent the multitudes away, He went up on the mountain by Himself to pray . . ." Matthew 14:23

Now in the morning, having risen a long while before daylight, He went out and departed to a solitary place; and there He prayed. Mark 1:35

Jesus, perfect and sinless, fully God and fully man, felt the need to pray, and He prayed often. How much more should we, imperfect and sinful, be found praying? Prayer is such an important source of power in our spiritual life because it connects us directly to the power source, God.

Jesus was extremely busy during His ministry years, so to ensure He never missed time with God, the Father, He often got up early and went to a place that was free from distractions. Jesus had many sleepless nights where He prayed to the Father all night long. If Jesus needed to pray all night, then we should be prayer insomniacs for God. If His compassions are new every morning (see Lamentations 3:22-23), then we should be up early, waiting for those compassions to arrive on our doorstep like the morning paper.

We don't possess even a fraction of Jesus' wisdom, discernment, or knowledge. We are light years away from approaching His perfect love, His inexhaustible grace, and His complete understanding. How we must crave prayer more than food and more than sleep! We walk in only a fraction of the power God has made available to us, and we pray only a fraction of the time our Savior modeled for us. There is no mistaking the connection.

So the lesson and reminder to us all is after you have prayed, then pray some more. And when you have prayed some more, then pray again. Make prayer the first thing you do, the last thing you do, and the in-between thing you do. Don't limit prayer to a few minutes during your quiet time, but let it spill over into all you do throughout the day. *"Pray without ceasing,"* as 1 Thessalonians 5:17 tells us. We live in a day and age in which we are hyper-busy. Our days are overfilled with activity, and I believe God often would simply prefer it if we would just be still, stop all the activity, turn off the noise, and just talk with Him and listen for His voice.

If you want to eat the ultimate breakfast of champions, it is not found in a cereal box; it is found in the Word of God. As the prophet Jeremiah said, *"Your words were found, and I ate them, and Your word was to me the joy and rejoicing of my heart . . ."* (Jeremiah 15:16).

There is great power in observation. The disciples spent three years with Jesus, watching His every move in every situation, and it dramatically changed them. We can learn so much by simply watching God work and move in our midst. That was the case with Peter and John, and it was evident to everyone who talked with them: *"Now when they saw the boldness of Peter and John, and perceived that they were uneducated and untrained men, they marveled. And they realized that they had been with Jesus"* (Acts 4:13). Spend time with Jesus.

Continuing On

Another thing we need to realize as we approach the subject of knowing God's will is that God often reveals only one step at a time to us. Rarely do we see the whole picture of God's plan and purpose for our lives. He may, at times, give us a glimpse as He leads us, but He always requires us to walk by faith and not by sight (see 2 Corinthians 5:7), which can be very unsettling for most of us.

We live in a day and age when we want to know everything and know it right now. Thanks to the Internet, we are a culture that transmits and receives information instantaneously. We can send information around the world in seconds, and so our tendency is to expect God to respond to us with the same speed. However, God does not operate within the confines of our expectations. As we learn to hear His voice, He will lead us all the way through this life and into eternity perfectly, one step at a time. He is ever-present, He is all-powerful, He is all-knowing, and He will guide us. As Isaiah 58:11 promises, *"The Lord will guide you continually . . ."*

Even though God has only given me one step at a time, I can look back and see how things have fit together as part of God's larger plan for my life. It is amazing to see how faithful

God has always been and how He has worked things together for a wonderful and glorious purpose, a purpose that at times I was unable to see or understand. Now I can see the path He was creating by all those single steps of faith. Many of the *Why?* questions I couldn't understand as I was going through specific trials, I was able to see their purpose later in the twenty-twenty vision of hindsight. Much of what was blurry has become clear, many questions have become answers, and seeing the road behind me has helped me to see the road ahead.

On this journey, we will seek to discover the will of God in our lives as we look to the Word of God so we can hear the voice of God and experience the power of God to walk the path of God . . . one step at a time.

2

Watch
THE
Road

∽

He who scatters has come up before your face. Man the fort! Watch the road! Strengthen your flanks! Fortify your power mightily. Nahum 2:1

The long and winding road of faith can be more straight and narrow if we allow God to direct our paths. God is not some cosmic being on some distant planet, completely disinterested in our lives. He does not hang a "Do Not Disturb" sign on Heaven's door, denying us access to Him. God is personal, relational, and intimate, and as such, He wants to have a personal and intimate relationship with every human being.

To borrow a slogan from the U.S. Army, God really does want us to be all we can be. Did you know that God created you—unique and special—and He has a specific plan for your life and a specific job He wants you to be doing as you serve Him? Ephesians 2:10 tells us, *"For we are His workmanship, created in Christ Jesus for good works, which God prepared beforehand that we should walk in them."* God has created us for a reason with a real purpose: a purpose worth pursuing and an abundant life worth living.

God isn't trying to play a cosmic game of hide-and-seek with His will for our lives. He isn't asking us to read the sun, moon, and stars like some ancient navigational system in an attempt to determine the path we are to take. We already have a built-in GPS, or God Positioning System, that abides within every believer: the Holy Spirit of God. All believers are given the Holy Spirit of God when they ask Jesus to come into their lives as their personal Lord and Savior. The Holy Spirit is our navigational system. The Bible tells us He is our Helper (see John 14:26) and He indwells us to help us understand, know, and apply the will, purposes, plans, and ways of God in our lives (see 1 Corinthians 3:16, Romans 8:9). As 1 Corinthians 2:11 says, *" . . . no one knows the things of God except the Spirit of God."* So, we need the Holy Spirit to act as our personal guidance system with God so we may understand the ways and the will of God. The Holy Spirit acts as our compass, which relates everything in terms of true north, which is Heaven. When we stray off course and away from God's direction, we should be able to hear the Holy Spirit saying, "Recalculating route," or "Make the first legal U-turn."

Often as Christians we ask these questions: How can I know what God's will is for my life? What does God want me to do in this particular situation? How does the Holy Spirit guide me? How do I know whether God is speaking to me? These are questions I have asked myself again and again through the years as I have walked with God. And as a pastor, they are also the most common questions that people have asked me, too.

All these questions have answers that can be found in the road map of life God has given us, which is the Bible. We can safely navigate as we allow God's GPS system, the Holy Spirit, to direct us.

As Christians, because we love God and have His Holy Spirit abiding within us, we want to do God's will, and we want God to be pleased with the way we live our lives. Moreover, we want to hear at the end of our lives when we stand before God in Heaven, *"Well done, good and faithful servant"* (Matthew 25:21). So it would be wonderful if our Christian journey were flagged with road signs that read, "God's will this way" with a giant, neon arrow flashing and pointing us in the right direction.

I have said to the Lord many times, "Lord, if you just tell me what you want me to do, I'll do it!" Maybe you have said something like that to God as well. I'm guessing there was no neon sign that suddenly appeared from Heaven, pointing you in the right direction. However, that is not how a personal God directs those whom He loves. He doesn't leave an impersonal road map for us to follow as we meander our way through this Christian walk of faith. Instead, He invites us to walk with Him and to become one with Him on this journey because He has gone before us and knows the way. And it is in the walking with God that we learn the ways of God.

So, how do we know where to begin this journey? It starts with a conversation with God in prayer and in His Word. It is here that we learn how to listen to the voice of God. You may be saying right about now, "Why is it that after I pray, I seem to expect to hear an audible voice from Heaven saying to me, 'OK, my servant, I have heard your plea, I understand the suffering you now endure and the answers you seek from Me. Go this way, follow Me, and I will now show you the great things I have planned for you.'"

But that is a Hollywood, Charlton-Heston-as-Moses version; it isn't reality. Just to be clear, as a pastor and disciple of Christ, I have yet to hear from God in that way (especially with a Charlton Heston voice). Nor do I realistically ever expect to hear God speak audibly to me.

So then, how does God speak to us so we can know His plans and purposes? There is no simple, one-size-fits-all solution for every person in every situation, but there is help and hope from the Bible. We can learn to follow God and to hear His voice by tuning in to the Bible and by allowing the Holy Spirit to teach us how to navigate along the road.

Often what many Christians struggle with is finding their place in God's plan. Part of the problem is our perspective. What we fail to see is what so often is right in front of us. We fail to take into consideration what God has already shown us about His will from His Word. Sometimes God doesn't *speak* the answer directly to us because He has already spoken it in His Word. That is why it is so very important as we approach the discovery of God's will for our lives, that we daily, diligently spend time in prayer and studying His Word. This will establish the biblical pattern by which God most often moves, works, speaks, and directs His people.

I am naturally a landmark driver. I remember how to get where I am going by remembering and recognizing landmarks along the way: a building, a store, a curve in the road. God's Word is filled with landmarks to help us find our way along the road that leads to Heaven. It will be much easier for us to get where we are going if we simply look for those landmarks in God's Word as we allow the Holy Spirit guide our way—and as we simply watch the road.

Learning from the Landmarks

What are biblical landmarks? They are those key people, places, and events that reveal to us who God is, who God created us to be, how we are to live for God, and how God wants us to relate to each other. With so many landmarks, we cannot possibly cover them all in this book, much less this chapter. So we will select and focus on a few landmarks that stand out in terms of how they teach us to successfully follow and walk in God's will.

In Genesis 37, we are introduced to our first landmark person: Joseph. A closer look at Joseph's life will give us a good example to follow and greater insight into the biblical pattern God would have us learn.

As we reflect and examine his life more closely, we will see that no matter what the circumstances may look like, God is always in full control. We will see God working both directly and indirectly to fulfill His great and glorious plans and purposes, not only in Joseph's life, but also in the lives of many who are connected with Joseph—some who cross the path of his life and others whose futures would be shaped, fashioned, and forever changed because of his life.

We will follow Joseph from the prairie of Canaan to the palace of Egypt. We will see him in a pit of despair and in a place of prominence. We will follow him to the darkness of a cold prison floor, where he would be wrongfully imprisoned and only later be righteously, rightfully exalted. We will see him tempted to sin, yet triumphant in victory. We will hear the despised words, see the effects of rejection and jealousy, and follow him to the place of being esteemed and accepted. Though the journey was a path filled with sorrow and much pain, through it all Joseph remained an example of how to follow God because of his faith and his conviction.

Young Joe on the Prairie

Now Jacob dwelt in the land where his father was a stranger, in the land of Canaan. This is the history of Jacob. Joseph, being seventeen years old, was feeding the flock with his brothers . . . and Joseph brought a bad report of them to his father. Genesis 37:1-2

The prairie is where we find Joseph, an ordinary young shepherd boy with an extraordinary servant's heart. In these first few verses, we get a preliminary glimpse into the character of this young man. It is a glimpse that will help us see the bigger picture into the how and why of God's plan for Joseph's life.

God's plan had started long before Joseph was even born, and that is how God continues to work out His plan in our lives today. The things God was looking for in Joseph's life are the same things He is seeking in our lives today: *"For the eyes of the Lord run to and fro throughout the whole earth, to show Himself strong on behalf of those whose heart is loyal to Him"* (2 Chronicles 16:9). God found a young man whose heart was loyal to Him, and it would remain loyal to Him through thick and thin.

Joseph's story isn't a tale about a tattler that ends in treachery. When Joseph brings a bad report against his brothers, it isn't that he is being a traitor to his brothers or breaking an unwritten code and becoming a snitch. When we look at the life of Joseph, it is important we not think he hated his brothers and wanted to get them into trouble. Rather, we need to see Joseph's dedication to the truth was tied to his loyalty to God, who is truth and thus was stronger than his family bond.

Joseph was willing to tell the truth, regardless of what the consequences might have been. You might be thinking, *Consequences for telling the truth? Absurd! Honesty is always the best policy, right?* Sadly, many didn't think so back in Joseph's day, and many don't think so today. No one can attest to this better than Joseph. A small, white lie here by Joseph would have spared him so much heartache, so much pain. However, this was not even an option for this young man. He was more concerned with doing what was right than doing what was easy. He made the choice to obey God rather than men, as Acts 5:29 says. It was a decision that would soon set in motion an evil scheme that nearly cost Joseph his life.

The story leaves us with only speculation as to the nature and specifics of what the evil was the brothers were doing. Based on what we see in Joseph at this young age and what we will see as we follow him throughout his life, it doesn't make sense to think that he is simply running home to daddy to tell on his brothers out of malice or ill-will toward them. He doesn't do that in Egypt when we see him reunited with his family. Joseph isn't using this as an opportunity to gain favor.

Rather, I believe Joseph separated himself from the evil his brothers were involved in and, as a result of not being with his brothers, Jacob would have inquired as to why he wasn't with them. Out of this conversation, Joseph would have felt the need to be truthful. It is also possible that the evil his brothers were involved in was so hideous that Joseph told Jacob about their actions, hoping his bad report might lead them to repentance. It is love, not hate, that seeks the best for others. And love, not hate, sometimes confronts sin in the hope a person will turn from it and be saved. This is the character of Joseph, and this should be our character in Christ.

If we brand Joseph a tattletale, then we must be prepared to place that label on Jesus as well. Every time Jesus spoke out against evil, it was done out of love in the hope that truth would bring repentance. True love desires the best for someone, and the best sometimes means correction. Jesus' confrontation of evil was done because He was holy and could not stand to let evil continue. He stood in direct opposition to evil practices in the hope that those who were practicing evil would turn from it and turn to Him, exchanging evil practices for holy living. As John 3:16-19 tells us,

> *For God so loved the world that He gave His only begotten Son, that whoever believes in Him should not perish but have everlasting life. For God did not send His Son into the world to condemn the world, but that the world through Him might be saved. He who believes in Him is not condemned; but he who does not believe is condemned already, because he has not believed in the name of the only begotten Son of God. And this is the condemnation, that the light has come into the world,*

and men loved darkness rather than light, because their deeds were evil.

One goal of truth as believers is to correct error; another is to set a standard by which we are to live rightly, much like a plumb line. The truth was given through the Law so we would know what sin is, giving us the ability to recognize our error, to see our sin, and to realize our need for God's grace and forgiveness. God's Word is truth, and in the New Testament, the function of truth through the Word is expressed this way: *"All Scripture is given by inspiration of God, and is profitable for doctrine, for reproof, for correction, for instruction in righteousness"* (2 Timothy 3:16).

Joseph spoke the truth, I believe, not to cause trouble or division, but that through the truth, there might be an end to evil. Living this type of life would mean Joseph didn't always have the best of relationships with others, and this is especially evident with his brothers. In fact, they hated him because of it. As John 3:20-21 points out, *"For everyone practicing evil hates the light and does not come to the light, lest his deeds should be exposed. But he who does the truth comes to the light, that his deeds may be clearly seen, that they have been done in God."*

If you seek to follow after Christ, if you are committed to living a life of uncompromising truth, then you eventually will find yourself experiencing a similar thing. Darkness does not welcome or even like the light, and we are told in the Bible that God is light, and in Him there is no darkness at all (see 1 John 1:5). As believers having Jesus living within us, we are the light in a dark world—a dark world of lies, compromise, and half-truths. And we are told if we are in Christ, then there must not be any provision made for darkness, because there is no darkness in Christ at all.

Choosing to live a life for Christ as His follower and disciple may not win you a lot of friends in the world. In fact, like Joseph, you can be guaranteed there will be many who will not like you at all. They will not like what you have to say or what you stand for, especially if your life of truth exposes their life of darkness. Joseph's brothers didn't want his light to expose their darkness, and they were willing to do whatever was necessary to extinguish that light.

Whenever you see God using someone in a mighty way, you always will see a person dedicated to the truth of God. Joseph was dedicated to following the truth of God in his life, he was willing to stand for the truth, and he was willing to speak the truth. This put him in the perfect position for God to use him.

3

Follow
YOUR
Dreams

❦

Now Joseph had a dream. . . . Genesis 37:5

Dreams are important to us. Some may be the types that contain our goals and aspirations, much like those expressed by Dr. Martin Luther King, Jr. in his famous "I Have a Dream" speech he delivered on August 28, 1963 in Washington, D.C. Here is a sample from that great speech:

> *I have a dream that one day this nation will rise up and live out the true meaning of its creed: 'We hold these truths to be self-evident: that all men are created equal.'*
>
> *I have a dream that one day on the red hills of Georgia the sons of former slaves and the sons of former slave owners will be able to sit down together at a table of brotherhood.*

I have a dream that one day even the state of Mississippi, a desert state, sweltering with the heat of injustice and oppression, will be transformed into an oasis of freedom and justice.

I have a dream that my four children will one day live in a nation where they will not be judged by the color of their skin but by the content of their character.

I have a dream today. [2]

Other dreams may be those that contain the regular images that pass the hours of darkness, night after night. Dreams are necessary. They help to keep a person from going crazy. If you doubt that dreams are necessary to keep you sane, then just try going three or four days without sleep and tell me you don't feel as though you are losing your mind.

There is a third kind of dream, however, and this type of dream is a rarity. But it is certainly the most significant type of dream, because it comes directly from God. Joseph had this type of dream—a dream that would cause others to think he was losing his mind, because when shared, it would turn his family against him. It was a dream that revealed the plan and purposes of God:

Now Joseph had a dream, and he told it to his brothers; and they hated him even more. So he said to them, "Please hear this dream which I have dreamed: There we were, binding sheaves in the field. Then behold, my sheaf arose and also stood upright; and indeed your sheaves stood all around and bowed down to my sheaf." And his brothers said to him, "Shall you indeed reign over us? Or shall you indeed have dominion over us?" So they hated him even more for his dreams and for his words. Then he dreamed still another dream and told it to his brothers, and said, "Look, I have dreamed another dream. And this time, the sun, the moon, and the eleven stars bowed down to me." So he told it to his father and his brothers; and his father rebuked him and said to him, "What is this dream that you have dreamed? Shall your mother and I and your brothers indeed come to bow down to the earth before you?" And his brothers envied him, but his father kept the matter in mind. Genesis 37:5-11

God had a wonderful plan for Joseph, and He decided to reveal a portion of it to Joseph in a dream. Although Joseph did not know the exact details of the plan, there was a basic meaning evident to everyone. The dream meant Joseph would have authority over his brothers, and yes, he would also even have authority over his father and mother. The dream spoke of how *all* would bow down to little Joseph. Everyone understood that. They were all clear on this fact, which is evidenced by his brother's jealous response in verse 8: *"Shall you indeed reign over us? Or shall you indeed have dominion over us?"*

But how would this come to pass? When would this happen? Would it be in a month? Perhaps in a year, would the tables turn? Even more intriguing, why would this happen at all? For now, these and other questions would remain a mystery to Joseph and his family.

Looking at this section in Scripture, it raises a logical question as we seek to ever make personal application of God's Word to our lives today. That question simply is, "Does God still use dreams to speak and direct His people today?"

Throughout Scripture, God has chosen, at various times and with various people, to reveal His will and His plans for the future through dreams. Joseph, as we see, is one such person. (Some other examples can be found in Genesis 20:3; 31:10; 40:5; Daniel 2, 4; Matthew 1:20; 2:12; 27:19; and Acts 2:17). The last book of the Bible, Revelation, not only by its title but also through its content, gives the longest and most detailed account of a revelation of God's plan through dreams and visions as the Apostle John records what God gave him to reveal about His will for the future, and more specifically *the last days* (see 2 Timothy 3:1).

Personally, I would welcome this form of communication from the Father, but I have not experienced it nor do I ever expect to. I do know several people who have had dreams or visions they claim were given to them by the Lord, and those dreams or visions proved to be true and accurate accounts of something God was going to do in their lives. There is no biblical indication that God has stopped communicating to His people or through His people in this way. As a matter of fact, Luke reminds us in Acts 2 of Peter's message at Pentecost, which in part said, *"And it shall come to pass in the last days, says God, that I will pour out of My Spirit on all flesh; your sons and your daughters shall prophesy, your young men shall see visions, your old men shall dream dreams"* (verse 17).

We must keep in mind we now have the complete Word of God, the Bible, given to us, so the need for dreams and visions is not an essential to hear God. Certainly as it pertains to new revelation or new truth, there is no more to be given. God has given us His Word, and it is all-sufficient. There is no need for anything new to be added; it is all-sufficient to lead and guide His people today. So beware of anyone claiming to have a new revelation from God or a new truth. Proverbs 30:5-6 tells us, *"Every word of God is pure . . . Do not add to His words, lest He rebuke you, and you be found a liar."*

That being said, God can still speak to us as it relates to *how* He wants us to carry out His will personally. He did this with the Apostle Paul: *"Now the Lord spoke to Paul in the night by a vision, 'Do not be afraid, but speak, and do not keep silent; for I am with you, and no one will attack you to hurt you'"* (Acts 18:9-10). God can and may use dreams in the lives of some of His followers, but God never will give someone a dream outside the scope of His Word. You can think of it this way: God's Word is the revealed will of God, and so God never will reveal anything to us apart from His Word. So when determining God's will in your life, if it doesn't line up with God's Word, then it is not God's will.

Let me give a simple example. In Matthew 28:19-20 we read:

"Go therefore and make disciples of all the nations, baptizing them in the name of the Father and of the Son and of the Holy Spirit, teaching them to observe all things that I have commanded you; and lo, I am with you always, even to the end of the age."

If you feel God has given you a dream to *go*, but you feel He is showing you to go teach the importance of being a good person, that dream did not come from God. God doesn't call us to be good, but rather to be holy. Be cautious and stay within the boundaries of Scripture, because the greatest revelation given to men is God's Holy Word, and within it is all we need to live godly lives and to live in the center of His will. Any thought, dream, vision, or other inspiration that does not line up with God's Word is simply not from God and not His will.

If we remove Scripture as the standard, we open ourselves up to all kinds of trouble. As 2 Timothy 4:3-4 warns, *"For the time will come when they will not endure sound doctrine, but according to their own desires, because they have itching ears, they will heap up for themselves teachers; and they will turn their ears away from the truth, and be turned aside to fables."*

We are also given a rather stern warning against tampering with God's Word in Revelation 22:18-19:

For I testify to everyone who hears the words of the prophecy of this book: If anyone adds to these things, God will add to him the plagues that are written in this book; and if anyone takes away from the words of the book of this prophecy, God shall take away his part from the Book of Life, from the holy city, and from the things which are written in this book.

A good rule of thumb is to keep in mind that our relationship with God is not only in the realm of dreams, but in every aspect of our lives with Him. In 1 John 4:1-3 we are told:

Beloved, do not believe every spirit, but test the spirits, whether they are of God; because many false prophets have gone out into the world. By this you know the Spirit of God: Every spirit that confesses that Jesus Christ has come in the flesh is of God, and every spirit that does not confess that Jesus Christ has come in the flesh is not of God. And this is the spirit of the Antichrist, which you have heard was coming, and is now already in the world.

This not only will help you discern whether you have received a dream from God, but also whether a teaching, doctrine, or other belief is from God.

Moving Among Us

As we examine this first portion of Joseph's life, we can see how God can move in our midst through the natural events in life to bring about His supernatural purposes. In many ways, we find that God delights in using the ordinary and everyday to show himself extraordinary. God was in the forming stage with Joseph and was preparing things for his future that were still a mystery to him and would have an unexpected outcome. Unexpected in that no one but God knew the who, what, where, when, how, and why regarding the unfolding of Joseph's dreams. It is like an artist's canvas before the painting is done. If we observe the painter from over his shoulder and look at the canvas, no doubt we will wonder what in the world is he is painting. Lines, colors, and shapes all seem to be unrelated and random in the beginning, but not to the painter. He already sees the completed picture in his mind, and with each brush stroke, he brings his vision to life. The whole picture becomes clearer.

So what did Joseph do to get God to give him this dream and to make him part of God's great plan? Nothing. Well, not exactly nothing. Joseph trusted the Lord with the little he knew and the rest he didn't know, because Joseph wasn't trying to get God to do something for him. Rather, he simply wanted whatever God had for him.

We can learn much from Joseph's simple trust, and especially take note that he was living an honest, peaceable life at the time, concerned only about his father's business. He wasn't crying out to God to be the second in command to the greatest leader in the world. He wasn't seeking to be the one that a nation would look to for counsel. He didn't set out to solve the world's hunger problem. He was doing nothing more and nothing less than seeking to live a life that honored God through his day-to-day living. Joseph's life purpose was to honor God, and this would remain the constant, guiding principle for Joseph throughout his life.

It should be a constant, guiding principle for our lives as well. As the Apostle Paul wrote to Timothy, *"Therefore I exhort first of all that supplications, prayers, intercessions, and giving of thanks be made for all men, . . . that we may lead a quiet and peaceable life in all godliness and reverence. For this is good and acceptable in the sight of God our Savior"* (1 Timothy 2:1-3).

Joseph was working in the fields, tending to the flocks, fulfilling the daily responsibilities of a shepherd. He lived one day at a time, but gave every hour of every day to God. He lived in obedience to God, which was demonstrated through simple acts of trust and faith. Joseph lived to please God and not himself, choosing to rest in His plan, His will, and His purposes, knowing His outcome was the best one.

This is so simple, yet we can make it so difficult. Why? Why do we try so hard sometimes to figure out what God wants in each minute detail of our lives, when so often living in simple obedience to His already revealed Word would lead us to live a life that would be a masterpiece?

Pursuing Righteousness

What did it mean for Joseph to be a shepherd? Easton's Bible Dictionary tells us:

> *The duties of a shepherd in an unenclosed country like Palestine were very onerous. In early morning he led forth the flock from the fold, marching at its head to the spot where they were to be pastured. Here he watched them all day, taking care that none of the sheep strayed, and if any for a time eluded his watch and wandered away from the rest, seeking diligently till he found it and brought it back. In those lands sheep require to be supplied regularly with water, and the shepherd for this purpose has to guide them either to some running stream or to wells dug in the wilderness and furnished with troughs. At night he brought the flock home to the fold, counting them as they passed under the rod at the door to assure himself that none were missing. Nor did his labours [sic] always end with sunset. Often he had to guard the fold through the dark hours from the attack of wild beasts, or the wily attempts of the prowling thief.[3]*

As 2 Peter 1:3 tells us, in Christ we have all that we need for life and godliness. I am convinced if we make it our aim to walk in the power God gives us in Christ for a life of godliness, not only will we be able to see God moving more clearly around us, but we also will see God moving more clearly in us and through us as He works to accomplish His plans.

As we live for God and live according to God's commands, the natural result is we will experience God, we will see His hand moving, we will be moved by His Spirit, and we will be conformed into His image. And through this work within us, God reveals His will and His works in which He has prepared us to walk. God will move in us and through us in very ordinary and everyday ways as He works out His extraordinary plans that will far exceed anything we could think or even imagine.

But this all depends on our trusting and obeying His Word to us. If we don't make it our aim to trust and obey His Word, we won't see Him work in us and through us.

Joseph had a sense through his dreams that God had a plan for him and that God was going to do something unique and special. But because Joseph didn't know how the dream would come to pass or what it would look like, he didn't know what God wanted him to do next. Joseph may not have known what God wanted him to do next, but he did know God, and that was enough for him.

In the absence of specific direction, Joseph did what God would have us all do today: simply continue to pursue righteousness. When we don't know something about God, His Word, or His will, then always go back to what you do know about God, His Word, and His will. Joseph lived to follow God's will and therefore found himself being led by God, even when he was unaware God was doing the leading. He made godly decisions that moved him in godly directions. He sought to live by God's rules; therefore, God ruled his life.

This is the best way to pursue God. It is the best way to watch for His will, it is the best way to follow Him, to seek Him, and to learn from Him. As we make it our aim to do all things for His glory, to think, to speak, and act in God-honoring and God-glorifying ways, it pleases God. And it places us in a God-position—the sweet spot, the place where God can use us and work through us.

If you will indulge me for a moment, allow me to use an illustration from my favorite sport, surfing. When you are on a surfboard and a wave begins to move in your direction, you need to position yourself so you are paddling forward in the same direction as the incoming wave. As the wave gets closer, you must paddle harder to stay in the sweet spot. Then the wave will begin to propel you forward. This is the time for you to push yourself to your feet and ride the wave. Once you are riding the wave, you are in balance with the movement of the wave. When you have done your job to get into position, the rest of the work is done by the power generated by the wave. As long as you stay balanced, you will remain on the path the wave takes. But do one thing to disrupt that balance, and down you go.

As we place our lives in the proper position through godly living, God will come and propel us forward by His power, moving us along the path He has chosen for us to take.

Joseph was a good surfer, so to speak, because he continually placed himself in the sweet spot through godly living. God then came along and moved him in the direction He wanted him to go.

4

Detours, Obstacles
AND
Rough Roads

∽

"Yes, and all who desire to live godly in Christ Jesus will suffer persecution." 2 Timothy 3:12

There are many parallels between the life of Joseph and the life of Jesus. Joseph is often referred to as a type of Christ, as he shares many similar experiences that would similarly mark the life of Jesus: rejection by his brothers, being brought to Egypt to be spared from death, being falsely accused, sold for a price, loved by his father, becoming a servant, innocent, yet imprisoned, and many other such parallels. One final similarity is found in the pit. Joseph was thrown into a pit and Jesus was cast into the grave, but neither would remain there. In both situations, it was the will of God being worked out for God's greatest glory.

Joseph is about to experience an unfortunate and very sad moment in his life, one which is a clear attempt by Satan to stop the plans and purposes of God. But we need to remember that nothing can stop the plans of God, as Job 42:2 reminds us: *"I know that You can do everything, and that no purpose of Yours can be withheld from You."* It was true in the life of Job, it was true in the life of Joseph, and it is true in the life of every believer. This type of opposition was not only shared by Joseph, Job, and Jesus, but it awaits anyone who truly follows God.

The evil that Joseph would face was an attempt by the enemy to destroy him and put an end to God's perfect plan, ultimately a plan that was leading to the protection and provision of His chosen people. What Joseph was about to experience in the next phase of his life introduces the topic of spiritual warfare, something that those who seek to follow God and do His will also can expect. As 2 Timothy 3:12 says, *"Yes, and all who desire to live godly in Christ Jesus will suffer persecution."* And 1 Peter 5:8 warns, *"Be sober, be vigilant; because your adversary the devil walks about like a roaring lion, seeking whom he may devour."* This is an unavoidable certainty; a fact.

Dangerous Curve Ahead

As sure as the pull of gravity is upon all who physically walk this Earth, so, too, there is a pull of evil against all those who seek to spiritually walk with God. Satan is always trying to tear down and destroy God's people in a vain attempt to put an end to God's redemptive plan. Just as Satan entered Judas in the final moments leading up to his betrayal of God incarnate, no doubt Satan was present that afternoon when the brothers of Joseph were so filled with hate they were plotting his murder as he approached. Whenever we see direct attacks against God's redemptive plan, the enemy is not far away—and even more likely, he is personally presiding over the attack. Both Jesus and Joseph faced spiritual warfare, but in both cases God still was in full control and Satan could not do anything God would not allow. This will become even more evident when we see Joseph's dreams come to life.

Just a brief word about the attacks that come to the person who is following God's will for their life: the type of attack will be different for each person. There is no formula that will determine the length of time it will take a person to go through the fire of persecution, and there is no formula that can predict the intensity. For some, it will be extremely intense and can rob them of all they have, much like the trials Job went through. For others, the attacks may be less severe. What we can be certain of is they will come; the attacks, persecution, suffering, and trials are a biblical promise, but even in the darkest moments, God's mercy is greater.

The promise of suffering is not one of those promises we really want to claim. I hardly ever hear people saying, "Thank you, Lord. May I have another hardship, please?" Or, "What I am lacking in my life, Lord, is difficulty." And even though it isn't something we naturally seek to experience, it is an ever-present reality that God allows suffering, trials, and persecution in our lives. It is in these times we must also remember that God's intention for allowing them is always for a far greater good than we can usually think or imagine. Anyone who has been brought through a trial can attest to God's faithfulness to see him or her through that trial. This doesn't mean the reasons for the trial are revealed right away, but they will come. This doesn't mean that the trials will be easy to go through. Fire is always hot, and trials are always difficult, but the heat is necessary for the refining process to work. Whether we experience an attack of the enemy or a trial designed to refine our faith, God allows them all and has His sovereign hand on the thermostat. So be ready and keep looking for God in the midst of the fire.

Up to this point, Joseph had been experiencing some opposition from his brothers. Yet none of this opposition could have prepared him for the hatred he was about to experience, an evil plan that had the devil's signature all over it. What started as envy would rapidly turn into bitterness, and then lead to hatred, finally culminating in an assassination plot. Genesis 37 tells us the dark story of Joseph being sent out on a mission from his father to go check up on his brothers. Little did he know he would never return. Joseph's search for his brothers would take him to Shechem, the last place his brothers should have been due to the bloody massacre they led on account of their sister Dinah (see Genesis 34).

As Joseph made his way into town, he met up with a stranger who told him his brothers were no longer in Shechem, but had moved on further north to a place called Dothan. So Joseph kept on going and, as he approached Dothan, his brothers saw him in the distance and began to hatch a plan to kill him. If it were not for the intervention of Joseph's brother Judah, Joseph would have died that day.

> *Then they lifted their eyes and looked, and there was a company of Ishmaelites . . . So Judah said to his brothers, "What profit is there if we kill our brother and conceal his blood? Come and let us sell him to the Ishmaelites, and let not our hand be upon him, for he is our brother and our flesh." And his brothers listened. Then Midianite traders passed by; so the brothers pulled Joseph up and lifted him out of the pit, and sold him to the Ishmaelites for twenty shekels of silver. And they took Joseph to Egypt.* Genesis 37:25-28

What a bleak beginning. What a dark moment for Joseph after recently receiving such a glorious revelation from God, only to be betrayed for twenty pieces of silver by those closest to him. Joseph had just received a divine dream from the Lord; a splendid picture of the favor God would show this young man. Now that was interrupted by an evil plot spawned from sinful hearts.

Aren't you glad that we live in a much more civilized world today, a world where we can say such betrayal no longer exists?

When we step out to do the work of God today, it will all be happy trails and rainbows, won't it? No, not exactly. We all have had Joseph moments. Don't misunderstand. There will be joy as we serve the Lord, but when we decide to follow God, to live according to His Word, and to seek His will, we are not given a *carte blanche* exemption from attacks, hardship, pain, and suffering. We do not move around this Earth serving God unhindered, unchallenged, and unopposed. We tend to think *God won't let anything bad happen to me.* Or, *Bad things don't happen to good people! Good always wins over evil.*

Well, in the life of Joseph, we will see that some bad things do happen to God's people, but God was always with Joseph. He never stopped working. We must always strive to keep an eternal perspective. The big picture is so vital in seeing how God works. It is the only way we can see clearly how God can work, does work, and will work bad things together for good purposes.

Imagine how helpful it would be if we could better understand the reasons for the trials in our lives. This is a very common question to which believers seek an answer on a regular basis: *Why, Lord? Why is this happening in my life, Lord? Why is this happening to me or to the ones I love?* Understanding this answer correctly is essential if we are to live in the center of God's will, because without the right perspective, we can live frustrated, unfulfilled, discouraged, and even fruitless lives.

As we continue to follow the life of Joseph, God ultimately will answer the question "Why?" and will show how all things were working together for His good purposes, which always lead to blessing, whether temporal or eternal.

Joseph exhibited a willingness to do the will of his father, without hesitation. His love for his father gave him a willing desire to live in obedience. The relationship between Joseph and Jacob shows us an aspect of the relationship between God, the Father and Jesus, the Son. Both Joseph and Jesus were sent by their

Father on a mission of mercy, grace, and love, and both learned obedience through suffering and through their willingness to do their Father's will, their Father's way.

A surrendered will is an important ingredient in the recipe of faith as we seek to serve the Lord and discover His providential leading. In order to do this, we must will to be made willing. Willingness means we are ready to act and to respond without hesitation, to respond with obedience to the commands of our Father. Joseph responds with obedience here by saying, *"Here I am"* (Genesis 37:13). When we hear the voice of the Father, we need to have a heart like Joseph's, one that says to the call of God, "Here I am"—not a heart that says "Here I am not . . . send someone else."

One of Life's Potholes

Joseph set out on his journey, only to find that his brothers were not in Shechem where they were supposed to be, but they had gone further out, past Shechem to Dothan. So he continued on, and as he approached Dothan, his brothers saw him coming and immediately began to devise a plan to kill him. A plot seeded in the flesh—full of hatred, bitterness, jealousy, and envy—had begun to sprout, leading them to devise such a wicked plan. No doubt they fed off each other's evil emotions, working much like a riotous crowd that gains momentum.

Joseph innocently and unsuspectingly walked right into the center of hatred and betrayal. However, his brother Reuben intervened and persuaded his brothers not to take young Joseph's life, but to throw him into a pit. What a sweet brother. With a brother like that, who needs enemies? The brothers agreed and decided to toss Joseph into the pit. Their next act shows the callousness of their hearts: they decided to sit and have some lunch while they considered their next move. Amid the cries and pleadings echoing out from the pit, these brothers felt no remorse and no repentance, but in their hard-heartedness, lunch sounded good to them.

All of a sudden, Judah saw an opportunity to make a small fortune off Joseph's misfortune and convinced the rest of his sordid band of brothers to make some quick cash. There was a traveling caravan of traders coming their way. Envy, according to the dictionary, is defined as "Painful or resentful awareness of an advantage enjoyed by another joined with a desire to possess the same advantage."[4] Webster hit the nail on the head, as Joseph's brothers wanted what Joseph had: their father's affection. And if they couldn't have it, then no one should. So the decision was made, the die was cast, and all were in agreement that they would get rid of the one who enjoyed the favor of their father.

Acts 7:9 tells us that envy was behind the sinister plot: *"And the patriarchs, becoming envious, sold Joseph into Egypt . . ."* What a short and sad sentence. How can this be God's will? Why wouldn't God intervene and stop such an atrocity against the only one in the family who seemed to be really dedicated to seeking God? *Why, God?*

Scripture doesn't tell us what Joseph was doing while he was in that damp, dark, and dirty pit as he was witnessing the exchange of money for his freedom. Perhaps in his naiveté, when it came to knowing his brothers feelings toward him, he cried out in a final, albeit futile, attempt to appeal to any shred of humanity his brothers might have possessed. Joseph, with increasing anxiety, must have been hoping all this was either a horrible joke or a bad dream and that any moment, his brothers would pull him out, or he would awaken from this nightmare.

You can almost hear him saying, "Come on, guys! Let me out! Very funny! I won't tell Dad if you just let me go." Or, "I promise if you just get me out of here, I'll leave you alone from here on out . . . I'll never bother you again . . . You'll never have to see me again. Just don't do this." But whatever pleas may have been uttered in those dark moments, whatever promises or bargains were offered up in desperation, they fell on deaf ears. What a sad scene.

Interestingly though, however natural those pleas sound to us, however human, however normal they might be, I don't think they were Joseph's response. Were there tears? Though Scripture doesn't tell us, I believe, based on ordinary human nature, that Joseph's heart was filled with sorrow, and his eyes were full of tears as he looked up from the depth of that pit at his brothers, seeing such hatred and coldness as his life was being bartered so cheaply. It had to feel as though his heart were being ripped out of his chest at that moment when he realized this was no joke. This was not a dream from which he would awaken, there was no getting out of this, and he would be handed over to slave traders.

What a scary and horrifying future must have flashed before his eyes at that moment. A future of unknowns now awaited him one thousand miles from all he was familiar with. Would he ever see his family again? What awaited him? Tears? How could there not be tears? How could there not be fear? But instead of cries of mercy for himself, instead of frantic pleas for freedom, I believe the nature and character of Joseph would have led him to pray, and to pray much like Christ would pray for those who were crucifying him: *"Then Jesus said, 'Father, forgive them, for they do not know what they do'"* (Luke 23:34).

Even as the Jews would mock Christ and show calloused hearts toward His pain and suffering, so, too, Joseph's brothers were callous, cold, and cruel. As insults were thrown at Christ by His mockers, yelling for Him to save himself, I can hear Joseph's brothers yelling, "Who is bowing down to you now? I bet you never saw this in your dreams!"

The enemies of God love to mock, but God will not be mocked. And although it seemed like a victory for evil, much the same as the Cross seemed like a victory for evil, that is not the end of the story: *"And the patriarchs, becoming envious, sold Joseph into Egypt. But God was with him"* (Acts 7:9).

5

Stranded

꿍

Now Joseph had been taken down to Egypt. And Potiphar, an officer of Pharaoh, captain of the guard, an Egyptian, bought him from the Ishmaelites who had taken him down there. Genesis 39:1

Where was God? Have you ever asked that question? Have you ever been in such despair that you cried out in wondering bewilderment, "Where is God in this? Has He forsaken me? Have I done something wrong to deserve this?"

The world often asks the question, "Where is God?" but they ask from a position of pride and disbelief as they look around at the condition of the world. They see the evils of poverty, war, hunger, disease, murder, and rape. And they conclude God must not exist, as if the existence of evil proves the nonexistence of a good God. Many mistakenly believe that if God exists, then His lack of action to stop these social and moral atrocities proves He isn't all-loving, all-powerful or all-willing. Basically, they wrongly believe that either He doesn't care or He isn't able to do anything about things here and now. Nothing is further from the truth!

These types of social problems do not prove God's inability to act or His lack of compassion for His creation. Rather, what it does confirm is the total and utter depravity contained within the dark heart of sinful humanity. Jesus experienced this kind of worldly logic as He hung on the Cross while a jeering crowd taunted him with statements like: *"If You are the Son of God, come down from the cross . . . He saved others; Himself He cannot save. If He is the King of Israel, let Him now come down from the cross, and we will believe Him. He trusted in God; let Him deliver Him now if He will have Him; for He said, 'I am the Son of God' "* (Matthew 27:40-43).

The crowd looked at Jesus, nailed to a wooden Cross, and felt this could not be the promised Messiah who hung there. They wanted to see proof, and they wanted to see that proof now. If God was working, they wanted proof then and there, because, according to human logic: *If God were there, surely He would put a stop to this horrific scene. If God were there, He would not allow this cruelty. Surely a God of love and compassion, a God who is all-powerful and all-knowing would intervene and end this torturous and bloody scene. God would not let His beloved Son, His only begotten Son, suffer in this way. Perhaps Jesus did something wrong. That is why He is suffering in this way. Perhaps He didn't have enough faith to get off the Cross, or maybe there is no God after all?*

As we go through difficulty, suffering, and times of waiting, we need to rid ourselves of the erroneous supposition that bad things don't happen to good people. The truth of the matter is God will never leave His children nor forsake them, just as He promised Joshua: *"I will not leave you nor forsake you"* (Joshua 1:5). So if God will never leave us or forsake us, then that means He is with us through thick and thin. He is with us when things are good, and He is with us when things are bad. He is there, just as the Bible tells us the Lord was with Joseph: *"But God was with him."*

In the most impossible of circumstances, on the days when there seems to be no light at the end of the tunnel, when it seems God is far away, we need to remember He *is* with us; He hasn't forsaken us. This does not mean because God is with us He always will reveal or explain to us what He is doing at that time. We are reminded in Isaiah 55:8-9, *"'For My thoughts are not your thoughts, nor are your ways My ways,' says the Lord. 'For as the heavens are higher than the earth, so are My ways higher than your ways, and My thoughts than your thoughts.'"*

SOS!

Where was God? Joseph's situation would cause most of us to ask that very question. Surely this couldn't be God's plan. Joseph was forced to work for a foreign master who knew nothing of the one true God. Slavery meant full obedience, and anything less meant punishment or even death. There were no slave unions. A slave was nothing more than property, and as property, a slave had no rights and often suffered harsh treatment. Joseph may have experienced some mistreatment in the beginning of his slavery, as most slave masters immediately would want to display authority and set the boundaries as part of a plan to break the will of a slave. This would be short-lived in Joseph's case, as he would soon rise through the ranks in his master's house. He was a slave with the golden touch. Everything he put his hand to prospered, but it wasn't Joseph's touch that was golden; it was God working through Joseph, because the Lord was with him.

Knowing God was with him didn't mean Joseph wouldn't have doubts, fears, or questions, but it would mean that through his trust and dependence on God, he would form a basis through which he could relate to God, understand God, and see God move. Joseph would seek to please God first in all aspects of his life, and by desiring to live for God first, the Lord would be pleased with him and use him to accomplish His plan. Even though Joseph didn't have the command of Ephesians 6:5-9 to follow, I believe he fully lived it:

> *Bondservants, be obedient to those who are your masters according to the flesh, with fear and trembling, in sincerity of heart, as to Christ; not with eyeservice, as men-pleasers, but as bondservants of Christ, doing the will of God from the heart, with goodwill doing service, as to the Lord, and not to men, knowing that whatever good anyone does, he will receive the same from the Lord, whether he is a slave or free. And you, masters, do the same things to them, giving up threatening, knowing that your own Master also is in heaven, and there is no partiality with Him.*

The desire to live for God in this way was in Joseph's heart and soul. No doubt everyone in Potiphar's house noticed this about Joseph.

Asking for Directions

So how can we know whether God is with us? First, God is omnipresent, which simply means He is in all places at all times. This means, in a general way, that He is always with us, because He is in all places. But this misses the personal part of the promise. God makes it personal when someone places their faith and trust in the Lord Jesus Christ. From that moment on, God gives us His Holy Spirit:

> *That good thing which was committed to you, keep by the Holy Spirit who dwells in us.* 2 Timothy 1:14

> *Or do you not know that your body is the temple of the Holy Spirit who is in you, whom you have from God, and you are not your own?* 1 Corinthians 6:19

God's presence becomes personal as He dwells in every believer, for it is God not only with us, but in us. What a great comfort to know the God of the universe dwells within me. What an intimate way for God to make His very presence available to you and me, and what confidence that should bring.

Joseph knew that God was with him, and he lived as though He were physically present with him. Everyone in Potiphar's household could see that something was different about Joseph. He worked like no other slave worked, and his attitude was unlike any other slave. Joseph wasn't a yes-man; he was honest, hardworking, diligent, and faithful. He always sought to honor God first, both from within his heart and then through his actions.

He carried this perspective even into his role as a slave master, where he likely transformed the way the slaves were treated. After all, he understood their perspective. He experienced their pain. He would have shared many of the same fears as they did. He was uniquely qualified to understand them, and he would do it all as unto the Lord, something they had not experienced from any other slave master in Egypt. The Lord blessed and prospered Joseph, not because Joseph sought prosperity, but because he sought to bring glory to God.

Joseph, in the dark moments of slavery, honored God by continuing to live the life God called him to live. He didn't turn his back on God or stop being faithful and obedient in living a holy life. If we want God to work in us and through us to accomplish His will, we need to remain faithful and obedient even in the dark days. We need to remember He is there and will work out His plan as we live a holy life.

It was obvious to all that God was with Joseph—so obvious it caught the eye of evil once again. Joseph's good looks and position of authority caught the eye of Potiphar's wife, and Satan seized the moment to try and kill Joseph a second time and put an end to God's plan once and for all.

It all began with the lustful looks Potiphar's wife cast upon Joseph. Time and time again, she pursued and propositioned Joseph to sleep with her. Time and time again, Joseph refused and rejected her advances. His strong faith was what convicted him not to sin against God and not to betray his Egyptian master.

Mrs. Potiphar, however, could only take so much rejection, and one day, everything came to a boil. Her passion was provoked when she saw Joseph in the house alone, and she decided to act. Cornering Joseph, she made an impassioned move against him by grabbing his clothes. Without a second thought, Joseph resisted and ran in the other direction, only to realize—too late—that his clothes were still in her hand.

Embarrassed for the last time, Mrs. Potiphar makes false accusations against Joseph and accuses him of attempted rape, forcing her husband to respond harshly against his favorite worker.

The enemy is always looking to see how he can stop the work of God. As sure as the sun rises in the east and sets in the west, so it is with opposition against God and against the people of God. Satan does not want God's plans to succeed, and since God uses people to accomplish His plans, that means Satan doesn't want God's people to succeed. As you follow God's plan for your life, you will face those moments when the enemy will use the pressure of persecution, the trick of temptation, or clever compromise to get you to move away from God's path. Satan may attempt to ensnare you in sin or discourage you so you walk away from the work of God. The enemy may even level an attack against your physical health. Just know this so you can understand the signs.

Reading the Road Signs

One sign that you know you are walking the path God has for you is persecution related to your faith—not hard times or difficulties in general, which everyone faces—but something specifically related to your following God. Remember, " . . . *all who desire to live godly in Christ Jesus will suffer persecution*" (2 Timothy 3:12).

As Joseph was living a godly life in Pharaoh's house, persecution came his way again. The first attempt by Satan was to get Joseph to sin sexually. Naturally, this would have been a temptation for Joseph. He would have had all the desires and drives of a young man, and for him to have a woman continually making advances toward him must have made it difficult for him to keep from giving in to the temptation.

So what did Joseph do? Did he pray, "Lord, is it your will for me to sleep with Potiphar's wife?" No! Joseph knew this was wrong in God sight. There are some things for which you do not need to ask God's direction, and this is one of them. Whenever the issue is sin, you do not need to pray to God and ask whether it is His will. *It is not!* Joseph knew that to do this evil was to sin against God. Although it would impact Potiphar, Joseph recognized that sin is first and foremost against God. Even though there are often earthly consequences to sin, sin is against God and against His holy standard. Joseph knew God, and he was faithful to live a life obedient to God. Therefore, he didn't need to ask God whether this was His will for him. Joseph knew God's will in this situation simply because he knew God. Therefore, Joseph knew sin must be avoided at all costs. Just as the psalmist says, "*How can a young man cleanse his way? By taking heed according to Your word. With my whole heart I have sought You; Oh, let me not wander from Your commandments! Your word I have hidden in my heart, that I might not sin against You*" (Psalm 119:9-11).

Day after day, Potiphar's wife tried to wear Joseph down as she kept pursuing him, trying to seduce him to sin. Ultimately, things reached a boiling point on a particular day when Potiphar's house was empty, and Joseph thought he was alone in the house. But along came Potiphar's wife. She must have thought to herself, *Ah, here we go! This is perfect! No one is here. This time he will give in, and this time I will have my way.* But to her surprise and anger, Joseph refused her again. As she grabbed his clothes in an attempt to pull him into bed with her, she was unsuccessful, because Joseph had purposed in his heart not to sin against God. He ran out of the house, leaving his clothes in her clenched fist.

Joseph knew that to give in to this temptation was wrong. How did he know this? Joseph knew the Word of God. And since the Ten Commandments weren't given yet, there was no law to spell out the sin of adultery. But Joseph knew that from the beginning, in the Garden of Eden, God had established the marriage covenant and made it a holy union. Joseph would have known this, since from his childhood he would have been taught about God. So for him to violate the covenant Potiphar and his wife had through marriage would have gone against what Joseph knew and believed.

Then, of course, he also had the direct command from Potiphar himself. Potiphar allowed Joseph to have anything in his house except his wife, so for Joseph to break his word, the command of Potiphar, and also the Word of God as he knew it, would have equaled sin to Joseph. I also believe that because God was with Joseph, He would have used the Holy Spirit at such a time as this to minister to him. I believe this to be true because as God chose men and women in the Old Testament, it appears His Holy Spirit was given to them selectively and temporarily in order to accomplish certain tasks God had for them to do. David wrote, *"Do not cast me away from Your presence, and do not take Your Holy Spirit from me"* (Psalm 51:11).

In the New Testament, this changes at Pentecost as we see believers receive the Holy Spirit once and for all upon their belief in Christ: *"Then Peter said to them, 'Repent, and let every one of you be baptized in the name of Jesus Christ for the remission of sins; and you shall receive the gift of the Holy Spirit'"* (Acts 2:38).

Then the Holy Spirit works to guide us and direct us, as we see in John 16:13: *"However, when He, the Spirit of truth, has come, He will guide you into all truth; for He will not speak on His own authority, but whatever He hears He will speak; and He will tell you things to come."*

So it is possible Joseph would have had the conviction of the Holy Spirit leading him to flee from this sin as well. The point is he knew the temptation he was facing was wrong, so he ran from it. Fleeing from sin is critical to following God, because sin brings death. And if we don't flee from sin, but give in to it, we will inhibit the working of God in our lives that can result in spiritual and eternal consequences. The more we allow sin to control us, the less God will control our lives. Sin is the fastest way to be walking outside of the will of God.

That was strike one for Satan and a home run for Joseph as he resisted sin by turning and running in the other direction—without hesitation.

Divine Detour

The enemy, however, didn't give up so easily in the life of Joseph. Nor does he give up easily in our lives. Once defeated, he doesn't decrease his efforts to get saints to stumble. Rather, he increases the attacks. Satan would attempt to kill Joseph by making a false accusation against him from the mouth of Potiphar's wife. She had decided this time she'd had enough. This would be the last time Joseph would refuse her. Since her attempt to seduce Joseph had failed, she would use her mouth to lie. Since she couldn't lie *with* him, she would lie *about* him. Satan would move Potiphar's wife to lie, because he is the father of all lies. Jesus told the Pharisees, *"You are of your father the devil, and the desires of your father you want to do. He was a murderer from the beginning, and does not stand in the truth, because there is no truth in him. When he speaks a lie, he speaks from his own resources, for he is a liar and the father of it"* (John 8:44).

Mrs. Potiphar lied by claiming Joseph had tried to seduce her, and her "Exhibit A" was his clothes, which were in her hands.

Satan knew this type of accusation would mean certain death for a slave. Add to that the fact that the accusation was coming from a high-ranking official's wife. It all meant there would be no hesitation in finding a slave guilty and carrying out the swift execution of that slave.

But this was no ordinary slave. This was no ordinary man. It was not that Joseph in himself was extraordinary, but our extraordinary God decided to work through this ordinary young man. God was seeking to use the ordinary to show himself extraordinary in the life of Joseph to accomplish an extraordinary plan. That plan included the protection of one man, which would lead to the protection of one nation, which would lead to the provision of the one and only Savior of the world, Jesus Christ. The enemy sought to stop God's short-term plan, thinking this also would stop God's long-term plan. But neither would succeed, because God is greater.

As we look at Potiphar's response toward Joseph, we find it is anything but ordinary. One would expect punishment to be swift and severe against Joseph, meaning certain death without delay. Potiphar, in his position of leadership, couldn't afford to show tolerance for such a personal violation of trust from anyone, much less a slave in his own home. But we don't see him taking the expected action. Why?

Potiphar was clearly in a difficult situation, much like King Xerxes in the Book of Esther, and it made him angry. In Esther we read, *"But Queen Vashti refused to come at the king's command brought by his eunuchs; therefore the king was furious, and his anger burned within him"* (Esther 1:12). Potiphar faced public embarrassment, like Xerxes, and other possible repercussions if nothing were done. Potiphar knew Joseph, he trusted him with everything he owned. He saw his faithfulness, his fruitfulness, and his trustworthiness. He would have witnessed his honesty and integrity in action time and time again. Every report of Joseph from the other slaves, servants, guards, and Egyptians had to be favorable, but still, an accusation like this meant something had to be done.

Potiphar couldn't keep Joseph free from punishment, because that would be saying publicly his wife was not only a liar, but also an adulteress. All this would equal public embarrassment for Potiphar, and he was not willing to endure that, even if it meant he would be punishing an innocent man. I believe that Potiphar must have known these were trumped-up charges, but what could he do? Perhaps Potiphar thought, *How could she do this to me? How could she put me into such a position?* Potiphar would not have been ignorant of his wife's tendencies. With a house full of slaves and servants, word would have come back to Potiphar at some point about how his wife was behaving, even if he hadn't seen it himself (which I think is unlikely). To think this was the first time she made a pass at a slave or acted inappropriately in this manner is naïve, but Potiphar was a man in a high position, he was in the public eye, and he couldn't afford to have trouble in his house.

At the same time, everything about Joseph was honorable, humble, and honest. Was there a way to avoid embarrassment and still spare Joseph? Was there any way to spare his most valuable servant and still deal with this charge? What was his solution to this predicament?

Prison! Potiphar decided to send Joseph to jail. It wasn't the most respectable solution, but it would resolve his difficulty. He would not have to kill a man he knew was innocent, and at the same time, he would not be openly calling his wife a liar, thereby avoiding further public humiliation. This had to upset Potiphar's wife, because she knew the normal punishment was death. She would get rid of Joseph if he was going to refuse her every advance, or so she thought. What Potiphar and Joseph couldn't see was that God was going to use this situation to bring Joseph a step closer to fulfilling His divine plan.

Staying on course

Before moving to Joseph's prison experience, we should note something else, another piece of the puzzle as we are learning to follow God and seeking to live in the center of His will. At the time this all transpired, Joseph most likely saw no reason or immediate purpose behind being a slave and was unable to see how this was leading to the fulfillment of those great dreams God had given him while he was back in Canaan. This is where we find an important piece that helps us as we walk with God. Which one of us hasn't at some point wondered, *Lord, how can my suffering be good?* What we must see is that even though Joseph may not have known how God was working in this situation, even though he may have had no idea how being a slave was bringing him closer to seeing those dreams become a reality, he still trusted God and he still obeyed God.

Our natural tendency, if we had been in Joseph's position, would be to look at these events and to think forced slavery must be a detour from God's path, prison must be the end of the dream road, leading us to wrongly conclude in this case that perhaps we got it wrong. Perhaps we should just give up on those dreams. But it is in this moment the depth of Joseph's character is so clearly revealed.

First, we don't see Joseph in a state of worry and panic. He isn't frantically praying, "Lord, get me out of here!" as if to use prayer as a means to claw and scratch his way out of a difficult situation. His inability to *understand* the ways of God did not inhibit his ability to *trust* the ways of God. None of this is to suggest that Joseph, in the darkness of slavery and prison, never prayed or never sought God for the answers to the whys and the hows of His plans and purposes. Nor does it suggest that Joseph never cried out in anguish over his situation and his struggles. He was like us. He had a nature like ours, and these questions naturally would arise within anyone seeking to live for God.

It is important to note, as we examine everything we see in Joseph's life, at the end of the day, Joseph left the unanswered questions in the hands of God, knowing and trusting that God knew best—even though he did not understand. And in that truth he rested. This is the place in which all believers need to be kept when we face situations beyond our control and understanding, knowing that God knows, and God is in control. And we rest there.

Second, God was with Joseph. Just because God was not speaking to Joseph the way He had spoken to him back in Canaan did not mean that God had left him or abandoned him altogether. It was obvious to everyone around Joseph that God was with him and blessing him, even in the hardship of slavery. If others knew it, if others could see God's blessing on Joseph's life, then surely Joseph knew it in his spirit too. Joseph saw and remembered how God's hand was upon him, how God showed himself strong on Joseph's behalf in the past.

We, too, must also remember that God is with every believer as well. Wherever we are, whatever we go through, however we got there, there is no place we can go where God is not, because He is everywhere at all times, and He personally inhabits His people. We can say with absolute assurance as believers that God is with us and in us, and He will never leave us or forsake us. And if God is with us, then God is also for us—and who, then, can be against us? No matter how bad it gets, God is bigger than anything that happens to us. He is in control, and He is always seeking to bring about His holiest will for our ultimate good for His highest glory in our lives. So even in the silence, God is with us. He may not speak to us the way we want or as often as we would like or the same way each time, but that does not change the fact that He is still near and desires to direct our steps, take care of us, provide for us, and use us for His plans and purposes.

Joseph knew the character and nature of God. Even though he didn't know all of God's ways, he still found the best way to live was to trust in God's ways.

Third, Joseph's desire always was to please God. What we notice from his life during this period is he sought to be the best servant he possibly could be, because it glorified God. Obviously, being a slave was not Joseph's choice. If he were given the option whether to be a free man or remain a slave, no doubt he would jump at the chance to be set free. As we look at this young man's life as a slave, we don't see Joseph being contentious or complaining, divisive or difficult, disinterested or disobedient. Rather, in all things it was the exact opposite. We see compliance, respect, and obedience. He was a hard worker, diligent, always seeking to go above and beyond by exceeding his master's expectations. His desire was to bring glory to God through his obedience, trust, and submission. The result of that kind of attitude and action was God blessed him.

How much more would we see, how much would be made clearer, if only we, too, would seek to live a life in simple obedience to God as Joseph did? Let us learn our lesson from this man of faith and choose to live our lives as Joseph lived his. In good times and bad, may we always and in everything seek to bring God glory in and through lives surrendered to Him.

Consider these words from the Apostle Paul:

Do all things without complaining and disputing, that you may become blameless and harmless, children of God without fault in the midst of a crooked and perverse generation, among whom you shine as lights in the world, holding fast the word of life, so that I may rejoice in the day of Christ that I have not run in vain or labored in vain. Philippians 2:14-16

And Peter wrote:

For this is the will of God, that by doing good you may put to silence the ignorance of foolish men—as free, yet not using liberty as a cloak for vice, but as bondservants of God. Honor all people. Love the brotherhood. Fear God. Honor the king. Servants, be submissive to your masters with all fear, not only to the good and gentle, but also to the harsh. For this is commendable, if because of conscience toward God one endures grief, suffering wrongfully. For what credit is it if, when you are beaten for your faults, you take it patiently? But when you do good and suffer, if you take it patiently, this is commendable before God. 1 Peter 2:15-20

When God is our master, everything He allows in our lives is an opportunity to serve Him with honor and to show we are good and faithful servants. Joseph lived this way, and by living this way, he was fulfilling the will of God. Joseph made it his purpose to live rightly before God.

In the absence of God's specific will in a situation, we are to follow God's general revelation and His general will as we walk. We are to do good, no matter what. We are to do good, even when good is not done to us. We are to do good, because it is the will of God, and it brings Him glory. This is so important in discovering God's specific and perfect will for our lives, because if we are not obedient in the general things God has already commanded us to do—which are all part of God's will—then we never will be able to see and walk in God's specific and perfect will for our lives.

God may call us to do different things in life, because He has uniquely gifted each of us, but He also has called us all to some other things in life as well. God used Joseph differently than he used Moses (as we will see in the pages ahead), but part of God's will for both men was to trust the Lord and not lean on their own understanding (see Proverbs 3:5-6), to be obedient, and to live rightly before God. Part of trust and obedience is not complaining about every difficulty and hardship you face, but relying on God's strength and not your own. You do this by staying close to the Word of God, being humble, doing good, fearing God, and loving others. If you are in doubt as to God's will for your life, then start walking in the simple steps of trusting and obeying, and watch what happens.

Fourth, Joseph was committed to living a life free from sin. Avoiding sin at any cost was a priority, and it must be a priority for every believer. Joseph was not sinless, but he did seek to sin less. Romans 6:12 tells us, *"Therefore, do not let sin reign in your mortal body, that you should obey it in its lusts."* We see this truth exemplified by Joseph's refusal to commit adultery with Potiphar's wife. Joseph was so committed to avoiding sin that he fled the tempting scene of seduction with Potiphar's wife by leaving his clothes behind.

God is well-pleased when we run from sin, and Joseph's response to temptation by getting out of Dodge very quickly was most pleasing to the Lord. We are not to linger around lust or casually stroll away from sin. Run! Turn and go as far away from sin and temptation as you can. Do not allow sin in your life. Make no provision for it throughout your life, and when you see the temptress coming to try and seduce you to do something you know is wrong, *run* as fast as you can. *Run.* Don't look back— run! This is God's will for you and me: to resist sin. *"For this is the will of God,"* 1Thessalonians 4:3 tells us, *"your sanctification: that you should abstain from sexual immorality."*

And the Apostle Paul gives us this warning about sin in Romans 6: 11-13:

> *Likewise you also, reckon yourselves to be dead indeed to sin, but alive to God in Christ Jesus our Lord. Therefore do not let sin reign in your mortal body, that you should obey it in its lusts. And do not present your members*

as instruments of unrighteousness to sin, but present yourselves to God as being alive from the dead, and your members as instruments of righteousness to God.

God is always seeking to use people who are surrendered to His heart, will, plans, and purposes and are committed to living a life free from sin, no matter what. Are you that believer whom God is looking for? If not, will you surrender your heart to Christ and choose today, like Joseph, to run from sin?

6

Are We There Yet?

❧

*Then Joseph's master took him and put him into the
prison, a place where the king's prisoners were confined.
And he was there in the prison. But the Lord was with
Joseph and showed him mercy . . .* Genesis 39:20-21

Have you ever had one of those days when nothing goes
right? It starts when the alarm didn't go off, so you are
already late for wherever you have to be. Then, while you are
running late and are now on your way to your destination, you
hit stop-and-go traffic, and your car seems to have some sort of
magnet that changes every light from green to red. When you
finally get to where you are going, everyone wants something
from you, and you can't seem to catch a breath or a break. By
the end of this hard, rough-start, touch-and-go day, all you
want is a little rest and relaxation. But even at the end of the
day when you get back home, you find there is a pile of laundry
with your name on it. Or you have to make dinner, do dishes,

put the kids to bed, and take the dog out, all to get ready to do it all over again the next day.

As frustrating as those days can be—and are—we need to keep things in their proper perspective. Paul was able to say after being beaten, stoned, imprisoned, and more (see 2 Corinthians 11:23-33 for more complete list of Paul's sufferings), these were small hardships:

> *For our light affliction, which is but for a moment, is working for us a far more exceeding and eternal weight of glory, while we do not look at the things which are seen, but at the things which are not seen. For the things which are seen are temporary, but the things which are not seen are eternal.* 2 Corinthians 4:17-18

We must always seek to look at life through the lens of the eternal in the temporal days of this life. God is always at work, even in those crazy days, and He is doing an eternal work through them.

Joseph had some crazy years. After being sold into slavery by his own flesh and blood and living as a slave for at least ten years, it seemed his life was going from bad to worse. Being falsely accused, he was sentenced to prison for a crime he didn't commit. This innocent man who was falsely accused now finds himself unjustly punished and imprisoned, cut off from the rest of civilization. Confined and caged, he remained a stranger in a strange land; yet God was still with him.

That first night in prison had to be full of darkness and despair. This new environment full of rancid smells, rotten men, and rats would be his home for the next few years. In the darkness of that first night, I believe one of Joseph's prayers would have sounded something like this: "Lord, let your light shine on me in this place."

Sure enough, God was shining on Joseph, even when he was in the shadows of an Egyptian prison, surrounded by the blackness of men's hearts. Despite the darkness that was all around Egypt and within the confines of Joseph's prison walls, God was still working. God was working out a brighter, more glorious plan with an outcome beyond those walls. The method God was using was still a mystery to Joseph, as are all God's eternal plans in the life of every believer.

Joseph, however, remained faithful, even when he was in the midst of a dark, concentric maze of the hows of God's will. As Joseph continued his commitment to faithful obedience, it became obvious to all those around Joseph that God was—and always would be—with him. God used this time for His divine purposes and eternal plans in the lives of others around Joseph—people whom God saw and desired would know Him; people in whose lives He wanted to work.

A Marathon, Not A Sprint

Such would be the case in the life of one of Joseph's prison guards (whom we would call the warden). He would seek to capitalize from the blessing of God's hand on Joseph. He must have thought to himself, *If God blessed Joseph while serving as a slave in Potiphar's house, surely he will bring blessing to this prison. If I give Joseph charge over it, we could be the best prison in all of Egypt. Maybe then Pharaoh would take note of me.*

I would suspect this prison did become the best prison in all of Egypt, because God was behind the blessing of Joseph. The warden, like Potiphar, became so confident in Joseph's abilities he didn't even look into anything under Joseph's care.

Joseph was living a commendable life in his new world. It is easy to do the right thing when things are going well, but can you remain full of integrity and do the right thing, even when situations are so dark you can't see your hand before your face? If you do, then you can rest assured that you are living commendably before God. As Peter reminds us, *"For what credit is it if, when you are beaten for your faults, you take it patiently? But when you do good and suffer, if you take it patiently, this is commendable before God"* (1 Peter 2:20).

Joseph had lost almost everything. He was without family, friends, and freedom, but he never compromised his integrity, his faith, and his belief and trust in the Lord, because he never lost sight of God. Knowing and following God continued to be Joseph's motivation and his meaning. It was also, I believe, his very sustenance during this desolate season in his life, much like Jesus, who said, *"My food is to do the will of Him who sent Me, and to finish His work"* (John 4:34).

Joseph remained faithful to do his best with all God put before him, all God placed in his hand, and all God allowed to go through his life. He was a trustworthy and obedient servant who was about to be rewarded for his continued perseverance. Not only would he see his dreams come true, he would also be made into the man God wanted him to be, which is always part of God's plan for our lives. When seeking to understand God's will and ways, we must never forget that He is always leading us into cooperation with His plans and conformity into His image. When in doubt or in darkness, remember He is moving us toward His plans, not our own, and He is working to make us a reflection of Christ. We are reminded of this process in the New Testament, when Paul reminds us of how God sometimes uses the process of conformity in our lives: *"And not only that, but we also glory in tribulations, knowing that tribulation produces perseverance; and perseverance, character; and character, hope. Now hope does not disappoint, because the love of God has been poured out in our hearts by the Holy Spirit who was given to us"* (Romans 5:3-5).

And Romans 8:24-25 points out, *"... hope that is seen is not hope; for why does one still hope for what he sees? But if we hope for what we do not see, we eagerly wait for it with perseverance."* Although Joseph could not see how all this was working together for his good and to accomplish God's plan for his life, I believe he held on to hope.

At the very core of our being lies hope. Hope believes, even when you can't see. Hope involves waiting on God with the expectation you will see Him act. Hope waits with endurance. Hope perseveres when you feel like quitting, because it is not a hope based on anything that is from you, of you, or comes about as a result of you. It is hope that is built on your relationship with the Lord. Hope anchored in the Lord remembers that God is faithful, and so you take Him at His Word.

The hope Joseph clung to was not based on his feelings, his surroundings, or his circumstances. Joseph's cause to hope was founded upon the word that God spoke to him through those dreams years ago. Joseph's hope meant that even though he didn't know the *how, where, when,* or *what,* he did know the *who—* God. It was because of Joseph's faith in and relationship with the living God that he was able to still believe that somehow and in some way, God would bring those dreams to fruition.

When it is God who makes a promise and plants a dream in the human heart, time is of no consequence, because we are not on our timetable for its fulfillment. We are on God's. And His clock looks at everything on an eternal timeline. I believe Joseph understood this truth, and because he did, it didn't matter that those dreams were now ten years old. They were just as real in prison for Joseph as they were the day God gave them to him.

The time had come for God to move another piece of the divine puzzle into place. In an interesting twist of irony, Joseph was about to be used to interpret the dreams of two men from Pharaoh's court, which ultimately would be used to fulfill the dreams God gave to Joseph:

It came to pass after these things that the butler and the baker of the king of Egypt offended their lord, the king of Egypt. And Pharaoh was angry with his two officers, the chief butler and the chief baker. So he put them in custody in the house of the captain of the guard, in the prison, the place where Joseph was confined. And the captain of the guard charged Joseph with them, and he served them; so they were in custody for a while.

Then the butler and the baker of the king of Egypt, who were confined in the prison, had a dream, both of them, each man's dream in one night and each man's dream with its own interpretation. And Joseph came in to them in the morning and looked at them, and saw that they were sad. So he asked Pharaoh's officers who were with him in the custody of his lord's house, saying, "Why do you look so sad today?" And they said to him, "We each have had a dream, and there is no interpreter of it." So Joseph said to them, "Do not interpretations belong to God? Tell them to me, please." Genesis 40:1-8

It is clear from the first part of this conversation that Joseph still was faithfully following and trusting God, because he began his response by immediately mentioning God. After being a slave for ten years and then a prisoner, he was still quick to point to God as the solution. Joseph knew firsthand God was the giver of his dreams, so he logically reasoned God was the one to turn to for the interpretation of dreams.

If you want to see how dependent a person is on God, how much he trusts God, and what priority God has in all aspects of his life, then look to see what his first response is in times of blessing and in times of difficulty. Luke 6:45 tells us, *"A good man out of the good treasure of his heart brings forth good; and an evil man out of the evil treasure of his heart brings forth evil. For out of the abundance of the heart his mouth speaks."*

It stands to reason if it is out of the abundance of the heart that a person speaks, and if God is in your heart, then you will constantly have God on your lips. It is in these immediate, knee-jerk reactions we can so often see what holds the place of priority in a person's life. No time to think, no time to formulate a clever response—only time to react.

And what was Joseph's reaction? God. God had the answer, because God *was* the answer. Joseph reasoned, who better than the one who knows all, sees all, and is all? Who better to turn to when you need understanding than the one who has no beginning and no end? Who better to act, to do, and to will than the one who is all-powerful? Yes, God alone has the answers we need.

Joseph's immediate response was God, and it also must be our immediate response as well. When we don't know what something means, when we can't explain something, and when we are left wondering about the whys and hows of life's circumstances, we always should know the who—God. God has the answer, and so we must look to God and His Word and ask God to reveal the answer to us, for it is in God's Word that all of the issues of life are contained. When we are in doubt, we must let our knee-jerk reaction be our only action, turning to God and His Word immediately. If we want to know the will of God, then we must continually turn to the Word of God.

Joseph's reaction says something else to us about his trust in God. His response and recognition that the interpretation of dreams belongs to God shows Joseph still believed God would bring his dreams to pass. Joseph fully trusted God would bring his dreams to completion; dreams that revealed his entire family would bow down before him one day. Joseph's resolve was that until he saw his dream fulfilled, he would choose to walk by faith, not by sight. His was a faith in God, faith in the Word of God, faith in the work of God, and faith in the promises of God—a faith that never disappoints, because it is all God.

Did Joseph have faith in God's existence? Yes, undoubtedly. But beyond that, he had a faith that knew God was in control, God was at work, and God was faithful to His promises. His faith in God caused him to be faithful to God. It was a faith that knows God will do what He says, a faith that knows God will honor His word, a faith that knows God will work things together for our greater good, a faith that knows God never fails, a faith that knows God is and will always be present, a faith that knows God will always provide, a faith that knows God has a purpose, a faith that knows God will show the way. This is a bottom-line faith that begins and ends with God alone. This is the faith Joseph had and the faith every believer is called to stand on in the darkness of whatever midnight prison we may find ourselves in.

Holding such a faith doesn't mean we know all of the hows, whys, or even the whens, but we do know the who behind it all: God. After all, if we knew or had all the answers, then there would be no need for faith. We must be men and women of faith who choose to walk by faith and live by faith, based on a relationship with Christ. It isn't enough to know God by name; you must believe in Him and His Word by faith, which is essential in the life of every believer. Hebrews 11:6 tells us, *"But without faith it is impossible to please Him, for he who comes to God must believe that He is, and that He is a rewarder of those who* diligently *seek Him"* (emphasis added).

We must not overlook the descriptive words God uses in this verse and those I shared just a few pages earlier. I am referring to words like *diligently*, *eagerly* (Romans 8:25), and *patiently* (1 Peter 2:20). Are they important? Are they there for poetic effect? Or do they actually carry with them a key to understanding the verse and its application?

Let me start with the obvious: these words are in the Bible, and that alone makes them significant, because every word given to us by God is significant and important. *"All Scripture is given by inspiration of God,"* 2 Timothy 3:16 says. Therefore, every word is significant, and because it comes from God, it should not to be overlooked or underestimated.

In Matthew 5:18 we read, *"For assuredly, I say to you, till heaven and earth pass away, one jot or one tittle will by no means pass from the law till all is fulfilled."* If God is so careful about His Word that even the dots above the letter *i* will not pass away until it all is fulfilled, then we can be certain every descriptive word used by God has been carefully chosen and is important for our understanding and life application. We can think of it this way: every word and every detail found in the Bible will happen exactly as it is written down, to the very last letter.

The words *diligently*, *eagerly*, and *patiently* are certainly descriptive, and yes, they do bring a touch of poetry, but they do much more than that. They give us insight into how we are to approach living for God. They help us with the direct application of the principle(s) God is communicating to us through that particular passage or verse. Often these descriptive words hold the key to the proper application. And at the end of the day, isn't that one of the main things we are truly seeking as we turn to God's Word? We want to know, "What am I to do with this, and how am I to do it?" This is essential as we seek to personalize the pages of Scripture and understand the will of God for our lives.

As we serve God, and as we respond to the situations life has for us, God is ever watching—not simply what we are doing, but more importantly, why and how we do what we do. In the above verse, Hebrews 11:6, we see that God places an emphasis on diligence as it relates to our pursuit of Him. We are not to simply seek God, but to *diligently* seek Him. That means we are to have a careful and conscientious pursuit of Him. It means earnestly and energetically seeking Him. When we seek Him with all our heart, soul, and mind, He will be found. When we seek Him with diligence in our daily living, He will be found because He rewards those who diligently seek Him.

Where the Rubber Meets the Road

I believe the diligent pursuit of God was a definite priority to Joseph, and that made such a difference in his life as he sought God's will. Sure, Joseph simply could have sought God (just as we can seek God), and that, of course, would have been good, but when we pursue God with diligence, it says so much more about the condition of our hearts. It speaks of a passion.

In Revelation 3, we find Jesus addressing a church that was no longer seeking Him. This church in Laodicea was reprimanded for being lukewarm in their relationship with God. We could say they lacked diligence in their pursuit of Him, and so Jesus said He would spew them out of His mouth. Our diligence speaks of our love for God, it honors God, and it brings Him glory.

Joseph's diligence can be seen in how he served in Potiphar's house. It was seen in how he persistently resisted evil, and we see this beautifully being played out by Joseph as he was quick to point to God as the interpreter of dreams.

Never grow weary in pursuing God. May your life be marked by a diligent pursuit of God, because when you do, *"He is a rewarder of those who diligently seek Him."* Who doesn't want to be rewarded by God?

Another important adverb directly related to Joseph's situation comes from our previous reference, 1 Peter 2:20: *"But when you do good and suffer, if you take it patiently, this is commendable before God."* Suffering for good was something Joseph was very familiar with, and here again is one of the keys to unlocking blessing through application.

What is application? It is recognizing truth and then putting that truth to use. So what is the application here? When it comes to doing good and suffering patiently, it has to do with bearing burdens, enduring trials, and not being hasty. I would also add that biblically, it would include enduring, waiting, and bearing all, with a sense of expectancy that God will work in and through every situation.

Staying close to God and waiting patiently for Him to work is important as we walk through this life and strive to discern God's will in the day-to-day of life. The only way we can expect to see God's hand working is if we stay close to Him, faithfully and patiently pursuing Him, knowing and trusting that He wants to work in our lives and will work in His timing and in His way.

Joseph gives us a good example of living in the center of God's will in the midst of some of the most difficult situations a person can face. Life is not filled with smooth roads, green lights, and express lanes all the time. There are many times when it is hard, dark, discouraging, and filled with trials and troubles, but it is during these times when the rubber meets the road that we need to look to someone like Joseph to see how to continue in the faith. By his example, we can see how the hand of God moved in and through his life so we can become better able to see God's hand working in and through us. Joseph is an example of someone who was used by God in a mighty way, but he also was someone who experienced extreme hardships before the will of God became apparent to him and to others.

Night Vision

So what do you do when things are dim? How do you follow God's path when you can't see in front of you?

Returning to the dreams of the butler and the baker, Joseph gives them the interpretation. First, the chief butler's dream is interpreted by Joseph, and he explains that he will return to the king's palace in three days, where he will be reinstated to his former position as the king's chief butler. After giving the chief butler the good news, Joseph makes a personal plea and asks him to speak well of him to the king so he might get out of jail:

But remember me when it is well with you, and please show kindness to me; make mention of me to Pharaoh, and get me out of this house. For indeed I was stolen

away from the land of the Hebrews; and also I have done
nothing here that they should put me into the dungeon.
Genesis 40:14-15

As soon as the baker heard the good report that Joseph gave the butler, he wanted to hear what his dream meant. However, what Joseph had to report was not favorable at all. Instead of restoration, he would receive retribution. In three days, he would be hanged for his treachery against the king:

Within three days Pharoah will lift off your head
from you and hang you on a tree; and the birds will
eat your flesh from you.

Now it came to pass on the third day, which was
Pharaoh's birthday, that he made a feast for all his
servants; and he lifted up the head of the chief butler
and of the chief baker among his servants. Then he
restored the chief butler to his butlership again, and
he placed the cup in Pharaoh's hand. But he hanged
the chief baker, as Joseph had interpreted to them.
Yet the chief butler did not remember Joseph, but
forgot him. Genesis 40:19-23

Before God would take Joseph out of this dark season in a dark prison filled with dark men, Joseph had to wait two more years—two years in prison for a crime he didn't commit. We are not talking about modern prisons with three meals a day, a room with a bed, the ability to shower, books to read, and even the opportunity to get a college degree. No, this would be a hole in the ground with a grate over the top. At best, Joseph may have been in a prison that was more like a workhouse, but either way, conditions were brutal and so were the people in them.

That's rough, and our first reaction may be that it seems to be unnecessary on God's part. But it gives us insight into how God chooses to work, and therefore it gives us a much-needed perspective into the heart of God. When we look at our own circumstances in light of God's heart, we see that He allows things to happen for the accomplishment of His plans. You see, when we realize God is more concerned with our character than our comfort, when we understand God cares more about advancing His divine plan than He does our physical ease, then we can begin to see our afflictions in the proper light.

We would do well to remember that steel is heated in the fire to make it moldable, and then it is hammered on an anvil. God often will allow us to be placed in the fire, so to speak, so we can be softened, purified, and then shaped into His image. If we begin to look at things with the perspective that seeks to find out what God is trying to do in and through our life situations, then we will be more likely to see His hand at work. Our eyes must be on God if we expect to see God work.

Most of the difficulties we will face in life pale in comparison to what Joseph went through, but his situation should serve as a good reminder that even in the worst of situations, God is still working out His plans and purposes in the lives of His children. We should never cease from searching to see His hand at work. Instead of our first reaction being "Why, God?" let's try saying, "How, God? How are you working in this? How do you want me to respond here and now in this moment?" We need to always keep in mind that even though we cannot see the entire road that lies ahead, with all its twists and turns, ups and downs, and hills and valleys, it is a road God has designed and will lead to His glory:

Therefore we do not lose heart. Even though our outward man is perishing, yet the inward man is being renewed day by day. For our light affliction, which is but for a moment, is working for us a far more exceeding and eternal weight of glory, while we do not look at the things which are seen, but at the things which are not seen. For the things which are seen are temporary, but the things which are not seen are eternal. 2 Corinthians 4:16-18

Making Good Time

Another question that comes out of Joseph's situation is another question that often follows "Why, God?" It is, "How long, Lord?" Now, it is important to note that we do not see Joseph ever asking this question directly. But it seems almost super-human if he didn't ask it within his own heart. It is here in prison we get our first indication that Joseph may be a bit discouraged and looking at the situation from his own vantage point. Who can blame him? In verses14-15, we see Joseph trying to take matters in his own hands as he seems to wonder, "How long, O Lord?"

But remember me when it is well with you, and please show kindness to me; make mention of me to Pharaoh, and get me out of this house. For indeed I was stolen away from the land of the Hebrews; and also I have done nothing here that they should put me into the dungeon.

David expressed these feelings in Psalm 13:1: *"How long, O Lord? Will You forget me forever? How long will You hide Your face from me?"*

And Habakkuk prayed, *"O Lord, how long shall I cry, and You will not hear?"* (Habakkuk 1:2).

In Revelation 6:10 we see the saints crying out, *"How long, O Lord, holy and true, until You judge and avenge our blood on those who dwell on the earth?"*

We ask "How long, O Lord?" in these types of circumstances, because we can't see the future. This, of course, makes it a little difficult at times when we are trying to discern God's will. We ask like David, like Habakkuk, like the saints in Revelation, because no matter how much we learn about God, He doesn't tell us everything. We often ask in moments of weakness. We ask when we doubt. We ask when we lack faith.

Joseph may not have asked the question directly, but his actions certainly speak more loudly than his words to reveal, yes, his doubt, weakness, and questioning faith. We see he is wondering how much longer he will be in prison as he explains his situation to the butler. He explained how he came to be in this prison perhaps in an attempt to manipulate the situation. Joseph was seeking to find his way out, but I think it was the anxiety of a broken man who was desperately crying out for help. And before him was help in the form of a butler. This was not just any butler, however; this was a butler from the house of the Pharaoh. Such providence must have been the Lord, right? Shouldn't Joseph tell his story after all? Who knows? Perhaps the butler can do something Joseph couldn't do.

What was the result of Joseph's plea to the butler? Silence. Two years of nothing. Joseph remained in prison with no indication that anything was happening. There was no indication anyone was trying to help him. No word from God, no word from the butler, no word from Pharaoh—just silence. That prison must have felt darker, damper, and more depressing than ever. Silence can be hard to endure. Solitary confinement in prisons is used for extreme punishment, and people have used silence to punish those close to themselves, through what is called the silent treatment. I don't think God was punishing Joseph in any way, but I mention these examples to show how silence can be hard to endure. If you have gone through a similar experience you know what I am talking about, and if you are going through a time of silence from God then you are probably wondering what to do.

So what did Joseph do? Did he try to make a daring escape? Did he try and cause a revolt? No, he did none of the above. He waited with endurance, patience, perseverance, and faithfulness as we are to do also. And I believe that in this place, he found his voice—not in the sound of his story told to any man, but from the depths of his heart, where no words can express, and only the ear of Heaven hears.

Lamentations 3:25 tells us, *"The Lord is good to those who wait for Him, to the soul who seeks Him."*

And in Romans 8:25 we read, *"But if we hope for what we do not see, we eagerly wait for it with perseverance."*

Then there is this familiar and encouraging verse from Isaiah: *"But those who wait on the Lord shall renew their strength; they shall mount up with wings like eagles, they shall run and not be weary, they shall walk and not faint"* (40:31).

The answer to the question of "How long?" for Joseph was about to be answered. The storm was about to pass. The warm sun was beginning to break through the cold. Joseph was about to see the ray of hope that would take him before the most powerful man in the world at that time, the king of Egypt. Joseph had been uniquely prepared to meet the challenges of leadership he was about to face.

As commentator R. Kent Hughes observes:

Joseph's preparation for leadership was in full effect. He was now graced with a sensitivity that was aware of and sympathetic to the plight of others. His demonstrated reflex was to first turn to God for wisdom and direction, which is essential to godly leadership. And Joseph tenaciously clung to his seemingly impossible dreams. He believed God's revelation. He knew what the future held. The brilliance of his leadership was firmly grounded.[5]

God told Habakkuk, *"For the vision is yet for an appointed time; but at the end it will speak, and it will not lie. Though it tarries, wait for it; because it will surely come, it will not tarry"* (Habakkuk 2:3).

Joseph's time had come! God was about to break Joseph out of prison.

7

Green Lights
AND
Blue Skies

⤐

Then the chief butler spoke to Pharaoh, saying: "I remember my faults this day.... Now there was a young Hebrew man with us there, a servant of the captain of the guard. And we told him, and he interpreted our dreams for us; to each man he interpreted according to his own dream." Genesis 41:9; 12

Flashing images! Strange creatures! Bizarre action! Racing heart beat! Sweaty palms! As you open your eyes, your first thought is, *What just happened? What was that? Was it real?* It was a nightmare. Nightmares can be so real and so vivid; they are hard to distinguish from reality. And it can take you several minutes to realize that what you just experienced was, in fact, just a dream. They can leave you dazed and confused and asking, "What in the world did that mean?"

Dreams were very important to the Egyptians. They believed dreams carried great significance with them and even warnings about the future. For this reason, rulers often would call on magicians or wise men in an attempt to make sense of their dreams.

Now Pharaoh had two dreams, and, simply put, they freaked him out. Seeking their interpretation, he called on his magicians, but they were unable to discern the meaning. As a result of their failure to provide an interpretation, God now used this to bring Joseph out of prison and set him before the king of Egypt:

> *Then it came to pass, at the end of two full years, that Pharaoh had a dream; and behold, he stood by the river. Suddenly there came up out of the river seven cows, fine looking and fat; and they fed in the meadow. Then behold, seven other cows came up after them out of the river, ugly and gaunt, and stood by the other cows on the bank of the river. And the ugly and gaunt cows ate up the seven fine looking and fat cows. So Pharaoh awoke. He slept and dreamed a second time; and suddenly seven heads of grain came up on one stalk, plump and good. Then behold, seven thin heads, blighted by the east wind, sprang up after them. And the seven thin heads devoured the seven plump and full heads. So Pharaoh awoke, and indeed, it was a dream. Now it came to pass in the morning that his spirit was troubled, and he sent and called for all the magicians of Egypt and all its wise men. And Pharaoh told them his dreams, but there was no one who could interpret them for Pharaoh.* Genesis 41:1-8

I suppose this was the first recorded case of mad cow disease. As strange as this dream seems, God would use this bizarre dream to move Joseph into a key position—a position that would set in motion the next phase of God's divine plan. Shortly Joseph would begin to see what God had been doing all these years, shortly it all would start to make sense to him. But at the moment, it was just another opportunity for Joseph to honor God through his obedience. Even though Joseph had trusted God every step of the way and clung to the dreams he received, he still had been unable to see the total scope of how God was orchestrating things behind the scenes and how long it would take:

> *Then Pharaoh sent and called Joseph, and they brought him quickly out of the dungeon; and he shaved, changed his clothing, and came to Pharaoh. And Pharaoh said to Joseph, "I have had a dream, and there is no one who can interpret it. But I have heard it said of you that you can understand a dream, to interpret it." So Joseph answered Pharaoh, saying, "It is not in me; God will give Pharaoh an answer of peace."* (Genesis 41:14-16)

The first words out of Joseph's mouth as he stood before the King of Egypt were, *"It is not in me."*

Wow! What an impressive and immediate recognition by Joseph that God is the source of all knowledge and all wisdom, and, in this case, the source of all interpretation. Just think for a moment if you were called in to see a very important leader, a CEO, or even our nation's president, and they wanted your perspective on something. How would you begin that conversation? Maybe something like this: "Well, thank you for bringing me here. I am glad to help and offer my services."

That sounds normal enough, but where is God? Where is the recognition that the only reason you have anything to offer is because of God? Joseph always was quick to point people to God, to let everyone know, "Hey, I am nothing without God." This is a consistent and recurring quality we see in Joseph and, no doubt, a main reason for God's using him so powerfully.

Glory Road

As we seek to gain insight into the way God moves so it will help us identify God's movement in our lives, we need to take special notice of these types of qualities in the people God uses.

From the first dream to the very last dream, Joseph always gave God the glory. Joseph knew beyond any doubt that the gift he possessed was given to him by God, and therefore God was the only one who deserved the recognition.

Personally speaking, I have seen God use men and women mightily who have displayed this quality. They recognize that *it is not in them*, just as Joseph knew *it was not in him*. They knew they did not possess the power, they did not have the strength, and they did not have the wisdom. Therefore, it had to come from God.

For Joseph, God received the preeminence, the recognition, and all the glory, honor, and praise. When we get this, God will work. All we have to do is remain faithful, and just watch and see what God will do.

After acknowledging the interpretation of Pharaoh's dream was not in him, Joseph declared, *"God will give . . ."* (verse 16). First, Joseph recognized that God is the source and anything good has come from Him. James expresses it this way: *"Every good gift and every perfect gift is from above, and comes down from the Father of lights . . ."* (James 1:17).

When the man or a woman of God is able to first understand that God is the source of everything good, including the gifts that operate in them, then they are ready for Philippians 2:13: *"For it is God who works in you both to will and to do for His good pleasure."* I don't posses anything in me or of myself that can make a difference in people's lives when it comes to the Kingdom of God. God is the one who gives us the ability to serve Him. Therefore, I have no right to boast in myself or to take the glory for something God has given me in the first place.

As Joseph stood before a king, he realized that he ultimately served a higher King. And as a loyal servant of the King of kings, Joseph began by rightly directing the focus to God, then trusting God to provide, and, in this case, to supply the interpretation.

Joseph showed a constant trust in and total reliance on the Lord, and he lived with the expectation that the Lord would provide. Joseph knew God was the provider of the interpretation for the king's dream, and He would bring it to pass, just as He said. In other words, Joseph trusted that God honors His Word. If God said it, Joseph knew He would do it. Joseph had an unwavering devotion and dependence on God's Word, regardless of the hardships he had experienced.

Can we say the same thing about ourselves? Do we believe God without doubting? When God says, *"I will never leave you nor forsake you"* (Hebrews 13:5), do we believe Him, or do we cry out, "Where are you, God?" as we doubt the very Word He has already spoken to us? Do we question His ability to provide and take care of our needs when He has said:

> *"Therefore do not worry, saying, 'What shall we eat?' or 'What shall we drink?' or 'What shall we wear?' For after all these things the Gentiles seek. For your heavenly Father knows that you need all these things. But seek first the kingdom of God and His righteousness, and all these things shall be added to you. Therefore do not worry about tomorrow, for tomorrow will worry about its own things. Sufficient for the day is its own trouble."*
> Matthew 6:31-34

We must believe without doubting—there is no trusting halfway. You either believe the Bible or you don't, and if you do, then you will put your full weight on it. If you trust a chair will hold you, then you will sit on it. If you don't trust it, then you don't. There is no halfway. We either take God at His Word, or we don't. If we don't trust the Word God has already given to us through the Bible, then how can we expect to hear anything else from Him? How can we be used mightily *by* God until we fully trust *in* God? How can we discover God's specific will for our lives until we discover the power and blessing found in what

He has already spoken to us? There is no mystery in so many of the promises of God. Oh, how much God could do in us if we simply trusted what He has already told us and just took Him at His Word! There is clearly a strength found in Joseph based on his total dependence and trust in God's promises. We don't know what went through Joseph's mind night after night when he was a slave or when he was in prison, but we do know that Joseph trusted God.

Right of Way

Consider for a moment the hundreds of *I will* statements by God in the Bible. (I would encourage you to underline them as you come across them. You will be amazed at all the promises God has made to us.) The question is, do we believe them? Do we take God at His Word like Joseph did? Do we have faith in His promises to us? A person can believe those promises are true, but never live by them. That is not a genuine faith. If we have faith in the Word of God and the promises of God, then we are living according to them, and we are living in full anticipation that God will follow through on those promises.

Allow me to illustrate: Say your best friend makes plans with you to go out for lunch, and he or she tells you they will pick you up at a certain time. Because you know and trust your friend, your actions will reflect the fact that you take them at their word. You will get dressed and do what you need to do to be ready on time, because you know your friend will be there when they said they would.

How much more are we to take God at His Word? If God says that He will do something, then we are to be ready for when He meets us for that appointment. When God says He will do it, then He *will* do it. When He makes a promise, He *will* keep it. We need to trust Him more and more and walk in the fullness of the promises He has given to us.

Faith does not throw a rock in the water to test it before stepping out of the boat and onto the sea. Faith jumps overboard and starts walking on the water. Just ask the Apostle Peter about that when you see him in Heaven. He has experienced both sides of that coin of faith. Why have faith in the Word of God? In Isaiah 55:11 God says, *"So shall My word be that goes forth from My mouth; it shall not return to Me void, but it shall accomplish what I please, and it shall prosper in the thing for which I sent it."*

If God says it, He will do it. Therefore, we must have faith in it. Jesus said, *"Assuredly, I say to you, if you have faith and do not doubt, you will not only do what was done to the fig tree, but also if you say to this mountain, 'Be removed and be cast into the sea,' it will be done"* (Matthew 21:21).

Fast Track

Because of Joseph's faith, God now gives Joseph the interpretation, and in turn, Joseph tells Pharaoh there are seven years of plenty and seven years of famine coming. Pharaoh is impressed with Joseph's ability to provide the interpretation, and since he was the only one able to give Pharaoh the interpretation, Pharaoh decides to keep Joseph around to advise him about making the necessary preparations for the coming famine.

Allow me to go to the highlight reel for the next few chapters in Genesis, because for our purposes, we are seeking more of the application as it relates to learning and following God's will in our lives.

1. *Elevated and Exalted* (Genesis 41)

This is one the most amazing parts of Joseph's story as he is elevated and exalted in Egypt. The king of Egypt recognizes there is something special about Joseph. That something special is the Spirit of God dwelling with him. The king then wisely decides that because the Spirit of God is with Joseph, he will make Joseph second in command. There will be no one with more power, no one with more control, and no one with more authority than Joseph, with the sole exception of the king himself. Joseph would answer only to the king. As a result of Joseph's practical leadership through preparing for the famine, all the surrounding countries would come to Egypt to buy grain. One by one, they all would make the journey to Egypt and stand before Joseph in order to buy what they needed to survive.

2. *God's Promise* (Genesis 42)

As God's divine plan was working itself out and as the dreams of Joseph were beginning to come to fruition while Joseph was the governor of Egypt, his brothers came and bowed down before him—totally unaware they were fulfilling prophecy, and totally unaware the governor was also their brother.

Joseph, on the other hand, did recognize his brothers and began to remember the dreams God had given him. All the promises of God must have come flooding back into Joseph's heart and mind like a tidal wave. It most likely was a bittersweet moment for Joseph as he saw God's faithfulness and his dreams being fulfilled, while at the same time experiencing the pain of remembering all the hurt his brothers caused him. But God's promises always come true.

3. *God's Purposes* (Genesis 45-50)

As the scene continues to unfold, Joseph doesn't immediately make himself known to his family. But when he does, he is both compassionate and kind.

> *And Joseph said to his brothers, "Please come near to me." So they came near. Then he said: "I am Joseph your brother, whom you sold into Egypt. But now, do not therefore be grieved or angry with yourselves because you sold me here; for God sent me before you to preserve life."* Genesis 45:4-5

Joseph began to reveal to his brothers the way God had been working, how God had been moving things in place for such a time as this where he could help them survive this famine. Joseph explained that the famine would be severe and last for several years, but God had been preparing the path for Joseph so when the time was right, he would be in a position to rescue his family. This salvation was not just God's favor for his family, but it also was actually a fulfillment of God's promises not only to Joseph, but also to their ancestor Abraham.

When Joseph's brothers returned to tell their father Jacob all of the events that had transpired in Egypt and how Joseph was alive and was the governor of Egypt, he seemed to be doubtful. It is in this moment of fear and doubt their father received the needed reassurance from God that all was well and this was indeed part of His divine direction.

> *Then God spoke to Israel in the visions of the night, and said, "Jacob, Jacob!" And he said, "Here I am." So He said, "I am God, the God of your father; do not fear to go down to Egypt, for I will make of you a great nation there. I will go down with you to Egypt, and I will also surely bring you up again; and Joseph will put his hand on your eyes."* Genesis 46:2-4

Part of God's graciousness is further demonstrated toward Joseph and his family as Pharaoh gave them the best land in all of Egypt. This allowed them to grow and prosper and fulfill another promise of God:

> *Now the Lord had said to Abram: "Get out of your country, from your family and from your father's house, to a land that I will show you. I will make you a great nation; I will bless you and make your name great; and you shall be a blessing. I will bless those who bless you, and I will curse him who curses you; and in you all the families of the earth shall be blessed."* Genesis 12:1-3

Then Joseph made one of the greatest statements a person can make, because it not only shows us his understanding of God's purposes in his life, but it also shows us the different ways in which God uses the events of our lives to accomplish His plans: "But as for you, you meant evil against me; but God meant it for good, in order to bring it about as it is this day, to save many people alive" (Genesis 50:20).

We are able to see the different things God may allow into our lives, what He may use to accomplish His plans, and how He may use the circumstances in our lives to accomplish His purposes in the lives of others.

All these seemingly independent and unrelated events should again remind us that God is faithful and God honors His Word. Over time, Joseph became aware of God's plan and purpose. He realized all the events of his life were designed to preserve life, not destroy it, and he was part of something bigger than himself. It was a plan to keep the children of Israel alive, but even more than that, it was a plan that would preserve the Word of God and the promise of God that through the nation of Israel, the Messiah would come. God wasn't just keeping the nation of Israel alive to keep them alive; He was keeping them alive to keep His Word alive.

As a result of the time the *family* of Israel would spend in Egypt, God would make them into the *nation* of Israel. God would use this time to protect and provide for His people while they grew, ultimately taking Jacob's—or Israel's—family of seventy and turning them into an estimated two million people by the time Moses would lead them out of Egypt.

Joseph was able to look back on all he had gone through—all the pain, all the hardship—and say the enemy of God was trying to do evil, but God, who is stronger, was able to use it all for good. But it was a good that Joseph could not see until God brought it to pass. Years of faithful obedience came first for Joseph.

Has God changed His ways? I don't see God operating any differently today than He did back then with regard to the revelation of His plans and purposes. We must walk by faith.

Final Thoughts from Joseph's Life

Joseph's life is a testament to God's faithfulness. It is a story of triumph over tragedy. It is a story of an enduring trust in the promises of God.

Through his life, we learn how important it is to be consistently living a godly life and how godly living will always keep us in the will of God, even when we might not be able to see how God is working.

Living according to God's Word is always a part of God's general will. Until we can say we are consistently doing that, it will be hard to see His specific will for our lives. This isn't sinless perfection, but a commitment to an obedient, abiding life in the truths of God.

Joseph is a good example to follow as he shows us consistent and continuous godly living in the face of uncertainty, trials, and temptation. The result was that God was glorified through Joseph and used Joseph to accomplish great things for His Kingdom.

Joseph had a belief in God, and his primary concern was to live a life that would bring glory and honor to Him. Joseph was an exceptional man of God who had a faith, obedience, and patience that we all can look up to and aspire to see within our own lives.

We need to be reminded that even when things may be at their darkest, God is still at work. As the saying goes, "It is always darkest before the dawn." Be encouraged, because just as sure as we are that, the dawn will come. So too, we can be certain that God's will shall come to pass. He has a plan and is working it out for good in our lives.

The following are a few Scripture verses that Joseph exemplified. No doubt, these qualities were instrumental in how and why the Lord used this man. We would do well to heed them, because they are part of the will of God:

> *His lord said to him, "Well done, good and faithful servant; you have been faithful over a few things, I will make you ruler over many things. Enter into the joy of your lord."* Matthew 25:23

> *Moreover it is required in stewards that one be found faithful.* 1 Corinthians 4:2

> *And whatever you do in word or deed, do all in the name of the Lord Jesus, giving thanks to God the Father through Him.* Colossians 3:17

> *And whatever you do, do it heartily, as to the Lord and not to men, knowing that from the Lord you will receive the reward of the inheritance;*

> *for you serve the Lord Christ.* Colossians 3:23-24

One of the key fundamentals that allowed Joseph to remain in the center of God's will was his faithfulness to God. Whether slave or free, captive or commander, everything was done for God's honor and for God's glory. If Joseph didn't believe something would bring honor and glory to God, he didn't do it. How much simpler it would be to live in the center of God's will if we made sure this was put into practice in our own walk with God.

Let us now turn our attention to another person whose life contains valuable lessons for us about living in the will of God: Moses.

PART TWO

❧

MOSES:
Walking and Talking with God

8

Are You
TALKIN'
To Me?

∽

*. . . God called to him from the midst of the bush
and said, "Moses, Moses!" And he said, "here I am."*
Exodus 3:4

Growing up on the East Coast, this expression was often
a part of daily conversation: "Are you talkin' to me?" If
someone came up to you and said something as friendly and
courteous as, "Hello, how are you today?" the normal reaction
was always, "Are you talkin' to me?"

The polite stranger would then be given a generous amount
of time to respond to your question, say one or two milliseconds,
whereupon the New Yorker (such as I) would then repeat the
question much more slowly, adding hand signals in an attempt
to help the stranger understand that you don't know them and
don't know why they are talking to you.

I can't say with any degree of certainty whether Moses looked
around at Mt. Horeb to see if there was anyone else around when

God unmistakably spoke to him for the first time, but I have to believe that in Moses' heart, there was the question, *Are you talking to me?* This was the first time God spoke to Moses, and Moses had to wonder, *Was He really talking to me?*

We can assume that Moses needed some further clarification, because in Exodus 3:6, the Lord tells Moses exactly who He is. Introductions are only necessary when you first meet someone. In our New York example above, if that stranger were to be introduced by a friend or were to have started the conversation by mentioning a mutual acquaintance, then the whole conversation would have taken a drastically different and friendlier tone.

When He talks to Moses, God doesn't dispense with the introduction, but uses an introduction to help this first conversation be received by Moses: *"Moreover He said, 'I am the God of your father—the God of Abraham, the God of Isaac, and the God of Jacob' "* (Exodus 3:6). Now God begins by mentioning some mutual acquaintances and builds some quick common ground with Moses by mentioning Abraham, Isaac, and Jacob. Once these introductions we are taken care of, God does not introduce Himself every time He speaks to Moses. Why? Simply because Moses had already been introduced to God, and Moses was now able to recognize God's voice.

In order for us to learn to hear God's voice speaking to us, we, too, must first be introduced to God. Certainly salvation is the place where we first hear God's voice calling us into a right relationship with Him, and it can be used as a basis for how we hear Him in the future. The first time we hear God speak to us, He may give us several confirmations so we will know He indeed is the one talking to us.

The first time the Lord called me, He knew exactly what I needed to hear so I would *know* it was Him speaking. During a conversation with a close friend, we were talking about a few different subjects, but our conversation eventually centered on one main issue. As I sought the answer to our discussion, I found myself opening the Bible. The place where I opened spoke directly to the very subject I was discussing with my friend. I had no prior knowledge of the Bible; I had never opened one before. I didn't know the books of Matthew, Mark, Luke, and John were called the gospels. I had no idea there was a New Testament and an Old Testament. But as I opened the Bible that night for the first time, God was there, choosing the pages. God was introducing Himself to me. He then began to give me an unmistakable answer to the question I had that night, and I knew in that moment, in that first conversation with God, He was indeed *talkin' to me!*

As we read through Exodus 2-4, we get a snapshot of how God reached out to Moses and began to interact with him directly. All the while, God had been putting pieces in place, leading to that first encounter. Events that were unknown to Moses were under the direction of God's sovereign hand. It would be years later when Moses would gain the insight through hindsight to see how God was divinely orchestrating these events. God was at work long before His first meeting with Moses. We will see God working this way often, working and moving behind the scenes while the person involved is largely unaware of the extent to which God is actually moving. This process is not limited to the first encounter a person has with God, but it is often the ongoing method by which God operates.

Moses' life breaks down into three main divisions:

I.   The First Forty Years: A Prince

II. The Second Forty Years: A Pauper

III. The Third Forty Years: A Patriarch

As we look at the life of Moses, keep in mind that we are considering his life from the perspective of how God worked in and through him to accomplish His plans and purposes, always seeking to discover how God wants to work in and through us to accomplish His plans for today.

"I Think I'll Have A Look Around:" The First Forty Years

It is unmistakable that in the first forty years of Moses' life, God had placed him exactly where He wanted him. God was directing Moses' steps before he could even walk. God was working to place him in the right place at the right time, because He had a mission for Moses.

Dr. I. M. Haldeman offers this insight into Moses' life:

"He was born in a hut, and lived in a palace. He inherited poverty, and enjoyed unlimited wealth. He was the leader of armies, and the keeper of flocks. He was the mightiest of warriors, and the meekest of men. He was educated in the court, and dwelt in the desert. He had the wisdom of Egypt, and the faith of a child. He was fitted for the city, and wandered in the wilderness. He was tempted with the pleasures of sin, and endured the hardships of virtue. He was backward in speech, and talked with God.[6]

God is often at work long before we become aware of His plan for us. We should begin to consider in our own lives why God has placed us where He has. I guarantee it is for a purpose. God has placed each one of us exactly where He wants us, because He has a special mission for us as well.

And a man of the house of Levi went and took as wife a daughter of Levi. So the woman conceived and bore a son. And when she saw that he was a beautiful child, she hid him three months. But when she could no longer hide him, she took an ark of bulrushes for him, daubed it with asphalt and pitch, put the child in it, and laid it in the reeds by the river's bank. Exodus 2:1-3

From here, Moses was discovered by the daughter of the king of Egypt, and she immediately took him into the palace and raised him as her own.

Moses had no control over where he was born. He could not control being placed in an ark as an infant in order to be spared from Pharaoh's slaughtering of Hebrew babies. Moses was not in control when he was found by Pharaoh's daughter and brought into the very household of the king who gave that order in the first place. Just in case you were wondering, God does have a sense of humor. First, the king of Egypt issues a decree to kill the Hebrew babies, then his daughter takes Moses into the palace to be provided for out of the king's resources, and finally, Moses' birth mother, Jochebed, is allowed to nurse Moses and get paid for it. That is funny. Little did the king know who he was taking care of, but God knew.

Prep Work

Moses wasn't being directly used during this time. What I mean by that is he wasn't actively and knowingly participating in God's plan during this period. So the question may arise as to why God placed him there. Why grow up as if he were an Egyptian, even though he was a Hebrew, in the best schools, with the best foods, lacking nothing, and wanting for nothing? Why? Well, first even though Moses was unaware of God's movements, God was indeed moving and using this time to do something important for Moses. What was it? Perspective! God was going to give Moses a lesson in perspective that would be invaluable to him during his future serving the Lord.

You could say this was the prep work. Before becoming a pastor I worked in the restaurant business as a chef, and most of the day in the kitchen was spent doing prep work: slicing and dicing, making sauces and soups, assembling product, and getting everything ready for service time. God had to do some prep work in Moses, and that began with perspective.

God moves us around in our lives and gives us experiences that help shape our perspective for the work (or service time) when God calls us to a specific task. It is all part of the conforming work, where we are being made into God's image. In the beginning, at the time of creation, God said that we as humans bear the image of God: *"Then God said, 'Let Us make man in Our image, according to Our likeness' ... So God created man in His own image; in the image of God He created him; male and female He created them"* (Genesis 1:26-27). Then throughout our lives, we are continually being transformed into the spiritual image of God. Romans 8:29 tells us, *"For whom He foreknew, He also predestined to be conformed to the image of His Son ..."*

God did not need to wait eighty years before using Moses. For that matter, God didn't need Moses at all. But God has chosen to work in and through His creation to accomplish His purposes. Therefore, it was Moses who needed to wait eighty years. It would take time for the prep work to be done and for Moses to be ready. God could have used someone else who didn't need that kind of investment, but Moses was the man whom God had chosen.

Something I have learned as I have been following God is that He is not in a hurry. His timing is much different than mine, because His clock is different. For God, a day is as a thousand years and a thousand years as a day (see 2 Peter 3:8). That's some clock! God will take as long as He needs to prepare a person for His work. It is much like on-the-job training. When you begin a new job, there is a period of time in which you watch, learn, and practice before you are allowed to go and do the job. Every job has a different amount of time allotted to this training. The same is true with God's training of a person. For Moses, his training would last eighty years. And even after the eighty years of preparation, Moses still would have much to learn both about God and about himself. But he would learn on the go.

Moses would continue to battle with one particularly hard lesson throughout his whole life: the issue of submission. The question became "Was God's plan going to be done God's way? Or, was God's plan going to be done Moses' way?" Who do you think won? On several occasions, Moses would have to learn the hard way that you must do God's work God's way.

Moses had a perspective in the beginning that God needed his help. There was oppression and abuse of the Hebrew people by the Egyptians, and Moses thought he needed to step in: *How can God do nothing? Doesn't He see what is happening?* Perhaps Moses thought along these lines: *Well, I see the problem, so I will do something about it. I am a respected man, I am an educated man, and I am a man of authority here in Egypt. I will deal with this myself.* This is where Acts 7 gives us a bit more of the story, which is extremely helpful as we consider how God guided Moses' life, as well as how He guides our own: *"Now when he was forty years old, it came into his heart to visit his brethren, the children of Israel"* (Acts 7:23).

How did it come into the heart of Moses? Simply, it was God. But just so we are not left to guess concerning the methods God uses, we must turn to the book of Nehemiah, where in the second chapter, we read how God was guiding Nehemiah during the rebuilding of the walls of Jerusalem: *"Then I arose in the night, I and a few men with me; I told no one what my God had* put in my heart *to do at Jerusalem . . ."* (Nehemiah 2:12, emphasis added).

God placed it in the heart of Nehemiah to go to Jerusalem from Susa in Babylon and rebuild the walls of the city. For Nehemiah, it all began with a burden God placed in his heart concerning the people of God and the city of God. God placed it in the heart of Moses to go visit his brethren. When he did, he felt a burden for them, as he saw how they were being mistreated. But Moses didn't respond God's way. So it was out to the desert for Moses for some long, one-on-one time with God. It took forty years for Moses to be in the place where God wanted him.

As I have recently turned forty, I can see how much I have learned over the years and how much more there is for me to learn. Although forty years sounds like a long time of preparation, I have a new perspective on that now and realize how short a time it really is. Whether or not Moses felt like those forty years went by fast, we don't know, but even after forty years of learning in Pharaoh's palace and another forty years learning in the wilderness, Moses still had much more to learn. You even could go so far as to say his real education was only just beginning at the age of eighty.

God wasn't calling Moses to action just yet, but to observation. This stirring of Moses' heart, I believe, was the unmistakable inner working of God's Holy Spirit, whereby God's Spirit prompted the spirit of Moses—or touched his spirit in such a way he felt some action was necessary. Some other examples of God stirring up a person to action can be found in Haggai 1:14 and Ezra 1:1.

It takes the Spirit of God to reveal to the spirit of man the plan of God. As 1 Corinthians 2:9-11 tells us,

> *But as it is written: "Eye has not seen, nor ear heard, nor have entered into the heart of man the things which God has prepared for those who love Him." But God has revealed them to us through His Spirit. For the Spirit searches all things, yes, the deep things of God. For what man knows the things of a man except the spirit of the man which is in him? Even so no one knows the things of God except the Spirit of God.*

Moses knew he was a Hebrew. Perhaps while growing up in Pharaoh's court, he was reminded, maybe even teased, that he was a Hebrew, because his people were slaves in the land, doing the work no Egyptian wanted to do as they built the Egyptian supply cities. Perhaps Jochebed whispered stories of the patriarchs in the ears of Moses while she was nursing him and helping to raise him in the early years of his life. No matter how much Moses walked like an Egyptian or talked like an Egyptian, he still was a Hebrew:

> *By faith Moses, when he became of age, refused to be called the son of Pharaoh's daughter, choosing rather to suffer affliction with the people of God than to enjoy the passing pleasures of sin, esteeming the reproach of Christ greater riches than the treasures in Egypt; for he looked to the reward.* Hebrews 11:24-26

Moses also was aware of his heritage. Perhaps during his younger years he may have tried to deny it or even ignore it, but he would be constantly reminded that his people, his Hebrew brothers and sisters, were still slaves in the land.

What He Knew and When He Knew It

One day the Lord stirred the heart of Moses to go and investigate their condition. God knew Moses needed to see the condition of his people with his own eyes.

Things haven't changed all that much for people living nearly 4,000 years later. Seeing is still believing. This was also the cry of the Apostle Thomas: *If I could just see the scars, if I could just touch the nail prints in the hands of my Lord, then I will believe.* So what did Jesus do for Thomas? He met him in his unbelief:

> *Then He said to Thomas, "Reach your finger here, and look at My hands; and reach your hand here, and put it into My side. Do not be unbelieving, but believing." And Thomas answered and said to Him, "My Lord and my God!" Jesus said to him, "Thomas, because you have seen Me, you have believed. Blessed are those who have not seen and yet have believed."* John 20:27-29

Jesus gave Thomas the opportunity to dispel his doubts and to move him from unbelief to belief.

God was giving Moses the same opportunity to go see and believe. Moses needed to see before he would believe things really were that bad for his brethren. Living in the palace of the king of Egypt, Moses had to have known about the slavery of his people, but until now he apparently never gave it a second thought. But the Lord knew Moses needed to see things firsthand for it to make an impact in his heart.

When Moses went to see the condition of his brethren, he was surprised at the reaction he received from his Hebrew brothers. *"For he supposed that his brethren would have understood that God would deliver them by his hand, but they did not understand"* (Acts 7:25).

Why did Moses think they would understand? Did the Lord reveal to Moses that he would be used in the plan of deliverance? We have no indication this was revealed to Moses prior to the burning bush encounter. So why would Moses think the Hebrew people would come to that conclusion? Did he think people would take one look at him, stop, fall to their knees, and say, "Hey, everybody! Moses is here to deliver us from the hand of the Egyptians!"

The Acts 7 passage seems to indicate that for some reason, Moses felt that when he took action against the cruelty shown to the Hebrew slave by the Egyptian taskmaster, others would see him as some sort of savior or deliverer. But he didn't get the warm welcome he had imagined. There was no ticker tape parade, no singing "For He's a Jolly Good Fellow." Instead of rolling out the red carpet, they reacted out of fear toward Moses. Perhaps Moses was thinking, *Well, I am the adopted grandson of the king of Egypt after all, and I have the power to make some things happen around here. I should be able to see to the necessary changes in order to help the Hebrews change their situation. I am somebody!*

Whatever Moses was thinking, we do not know, because the Bible does not tell us specifically. But we can clearly infer from this passage in Acts that he thought he was part of the solution. Moses had his plan, and he was going to get things done his way, but there is no mention of God in his initial plans. As we read in Acts 7, the focus was on Moses. It was going to happen by Moses' hand, not by God's hand. But any time the focus is off the Lord and placed on ourselves, it will always get us into trouble.

At this early stage, we do not know to what extent Moses thought he was to be used by God to deliver His people from Egyptian slavery. In the Acts passage we can also see a glimpse into the heart of God that deliverance would come under Moses. However, the when, where, how, and what methods God would use are not revealed. We do know that based on his reaction at the burning bush, it is clear that Moses had no idea of the full extent to which God was going to use him.

Moses had gotten the first part of God's plan right by going and seeing his brethren. During that visit, he was given a burden for God's people and their condition. This seems to be all that was placed on Moses' heart by the Lord at that time. What actions Moses took after that burden was placed on his heart were definitely all Moses'. We do not see him praying, nor is there any account of him having a conversation with God. All that we find is a 100-percent-Moses reaction. He not only reacted, but he also overreacted as he killed the Egyptian taskmaster. The Lord didn't tell Moses to do anything after checking things out. There was no command given to rise up against the tyranny of Egypt. God only put it in the heart of Moses to go and see. The most common way God will begin leading a person in the way of His will is a stirring in his heart and then a burden to first go and see.

Moses needed to have a change of perspective, one that would show him that all the wisdom of man is foolishness compared to the wisdom of God (see 1 Corinthians 3:19; Matthew 19:26). Moses needed an extreme perspective makeover, and the only way that would happen was through the process of waiting patiently on God. God wanted Moses to simply see the situation through

His eyes. He wasn't asking Moses to act on the situation, because it wasn't God's time.

Moses wasn't ready yet, even though he had accumulated knowledge from the most advanced country in the world, learning in the best schools and the world's largest library nearby, having access to all the latest in art and entertainment, and exposure to dignitaries and rulers from all over the world as they came to Egypt to visit the great Pharaoh. Despite all of these influences, experiences, and knowledge, Moses still knew nothing when it came to wisdom and understanding into the ways that God operates. Moses spent forty years learning the ways of the world; now he needed to spend forty years unlearning the ways of the world and learning the ways of God.

Check It Out

From tracing the pattern of God's leading Moses in these beginning days of their walk together, I have found a pattern that has been repeated as I have seen and experienced God moving in my life and in the lives of others. God begins by doing a stirring within the deep recesses of a person's heart and spirit. This often means a person will receive a burden for some work of God for the people of God, or to lead people to God. At first it is often just a feeling, perhaps a heaviness of heart concerning the spiritual well-being of others. It can be for a ministry in your church that already exists, it may be a ministry that isn't in place yet, or it may be a burden for a group of people in your area locally, within your own family, or in another area far away. There are many other possibilities, but the main point is the burden God places on your heart is a burden that is on the heart of God.

Then God moves by providing an opportunity for you to go and see for yourself, what you might call a check-it-out opportunity. During this time, it is important to spend much time in prayer. Pray before you go, pray while you are going, pray while you are observing, and even pray after returning. This is the time to be continually praying for God's wisdom, seeking His leading and direction for you specifically concerning this situation.

Pray before stepping out into ministry at your church with the same fervency that you would pray if you were considering leaving to go to a foreign country to do missions work. We should never be cavalier in our approach to the will of God. As you go and check things out, and if you have been praying through the entire experience, God will begin to reveal how to proceed, which is that next step. A burden will lead to action, but—and this cannot be overemphasized or overstated—God is the one who must open the door of opportunity for us to take the next step so we can be used. We must wait on God. Things must be done in His timing. We don't want to make the same mistake Moses made by stepping out ahead of God and trying to solve a situation in our own strength. Moses took matters into his own hands. He acted too quickly, not to mention in the wrong way.

God's main concern is with people and their relationship to Him. Therefore, all ministry should, on some level, center on people's relationship to God. It may be brought about by bringing someone into a relationship with God through evangelism, or it may be by deepening an existing relationship with God that someone already has through edification and exhortation. Moses' ministry was not just about being the one whom God used to deliver His people from Egypt; it was about their relationship with God. Simply put, they were not in a right relationship with God, and so God's main concern was returning them to a right relationship.

He wanted them to know that He was the Lord, their God, so He would send His people, the Israelites, into the wilderness for an education in relating, relying, and resting in a relationship with God. Any true ministry of God will focus on people's relationship with God. The two main aspects involve helping people to get to know God—salvation—or helping them to get to know Him better—growing in God.

Moses desperately needed to get to know God better so he could be used to show the people the right way to relate to God. Moses would be sent off to school for forty years at the University of Midian to earn his PhD in waiting.

9

Training Wheels

⤸

Moses fled and became a dweller in the land of Midian, where he had two sons. Acts 7:29

We don't know much of what happened to Moses during the forty years he spent as a shepherd in the land of Midian. What I believe we do know is he found contentment and humility during this long season of his life. Perhaps Moses found a type of contentment out in the field that he never knew in Pharaoh's house. But going from the palace to the prairie certainly had an effect on Moses' character, and no doubt it went a long way in teaching him the humility he would need to serve the Lord.

Seeing all the splendor of Egypt, the mightiest country in the world, couldn't compare to living out in the wilderness under all the splendor of God's mighty creation. Long, lonely days out in the fields with the herds of sheep certainly would be good preparation for the final forty years of Moses' life when he would be out in the wilderness, shepherding the children of Israel, leading them out of Egypt, and tending to them in their wilderness wanderings. God was preparing Moses through a hands-on approach, giving him practical life experience that would serve to teach and train him for what lay ahead.

This training, however, most likely was completely unknown to Moses during those forty years. As far as Moses was concerned, he was a shepherd in Midian now. No doubt his mind would often think back to Egypt, reflecting on his time there and trying to make sense of it all. We will give him the benefit of the doubt and assume that in this place, he sought the spiritual significance of where his life had taken him.

For Moses, his life as a shepherd brought him what he wanted, which was a simple, quiet life, something much different than the life he had known in Egypt. But for Moses, it also was an escape. Moses had fled in fear. He made the choice to run. It was his way of not dealing directly with the problem. And here we see a *but God* moment. The *but God* moments in life and in Scripture are among my favorite words, as so often they indicate a change in direction due to the direct intervention of God in a situation. In this season of Moses' journey is our *but God* moment as he meets God, timed in a special way in his life. Moses was finally ready, and now God would speak.

Moses had spent forty years learning from the wise men of Egypt, and now Moses would spend forty years under the wise instruction of the priest of Midian, getting a degree from the school of hard knocks. One lesson we will see that Moses learned was the lesson of contentment. It is a lesson the Apostle Paul learned:

Not that I speak in regard to need, for I have learned in whatever state I am, to be content. Philippians 4:11

And having food and clothing, with these we shall be content. 1 Timothy 6:8

It is also a lesson we must learn if we are seeking to learn how to follow God and are to serve the Lord without striving in our own efforts. Hebrews 13:5 reminds us, *"Let your conduct be without covetousness; be content with such things as you have. For He Himself has said, 'I will never leave you nor forsake you.'"*

Not only did Moses learn contentment, but he also learned humility during these forty years. It was a lesson the Apostle Peter learned the hard way as he walked with Jesus. The most striking example from Peter's life comes as he proclaimed to Jesus that he would die for Him, and then the same night, Peter denied that he even knew Christ. That would prove to be one of the most pivotal lessons in humility that Peter would learn, and it became the example from which the Lord also would restore Peter to service (see John 21). There also was the time when Peter rebuked the Lord, and the Lord's response to Peter was, *"Get behind Me, Satan!"* (Matthew 16:23). Ouch! That had to leave a lasting impression on Peter. Lessons such as these enabled Peter to write this about humility: *"...be clothed with humility, for 'God resists the proud, but gives grace to the humble'"* (1 Peter 5:5).

From the impulsiveness of his younger days, Peter learned humility. Moses was impulsive in his younger days as well. He had confidence in his own power and position, and he was self-confident. And all of that self-confidence is what led him into a forty-year-long lesson in humility. As Proverbs 11:2 says, *"When pride comes, then comes shame; but with the humble is wisdom."*

Driver's Education

As we come to Exodus 3, God is now ready to reach out to Moses. Moses has spent his second forty years being broken of his pride, unlearning the things his time in Egypt taught him, and learning about humility and contentment. Even though he still had much more to learn, he was ready for God to begin to slowly reveal His plan to His servant.

Please do not underestimate the importance of these two qualities: humility and contentment. I believe God would have waited another forty years if that's what it would have taken for Moses to learn these qualities. Whenever we see these two qualities in someone's life, we see a person do great things for God. Don't believe me or take my word for it. Just take the time to go through church history and look through the pages of Scripture, and you will see some of the great works done for God through those yielded to God. And in the person God uses, you will also invariably find contentment with God and humility.

What did Moses know, and when did he know it? That is the question. The simple answer is that we don't know exactly what Moses knew prior to the burning bush. Moses may have known he was going to be used by God. He may even have known he would be used to deliver the Israelites. But it is all speculation, and simply put, we don't know for sure how much Moses knew and when he knew it. What we do know is that when it was time for God to move, speak, and reveal His plan to Moses, He did so in an unmistakable way (see Exodus 3).

Now Moses had been tending to his father-in-law's flock, which led him to the back of the desert, eventually taking him to a mountain called Horeb. It is here that Moses had his first and most memorable encounter with God. God would appear to Moses in a burning bush, a miraculous sight where a highly flammable plant had a constant flame, yet it was never consumed by it. From the center of this continuous flame, God called out to Moses by name and introduced himself to Moses:

> *Then He said, "Do not draw near this place. Take your sandals off your feet, for the place where you stand is holy ground." Moreover He said, "I am the God of your father—the God of Abraham, the God of Isaac, and the God of Jacob." And Moses hid his face, for he was afraid to look upon God.* Exodus 3:5-6

As God continued His introduction, He explained to Moses that He had seen the oppression of His people and He had heard their cries. And as if to demonstrate His sovereign timetable, God revealed to Moses that now was the time for action. The time had come for the deliverance of His people, and Moses would be the one to take charge and lead the people under God's authority and direction. But as Moses thought about this daunting task and all the responsibility associated with being God's representative and God's spokesman, he needed a little convincing:

But Moses said to God, "Who am I that I should go to Pharaoh, and that I should bring the children of Israel out of Egypt?" So He said, "I will certainly be with you. And this shall be a sign to you that I have sent you: When you have brought the people out of Egypt, you shall serve God on this mountain."

Then Moses said to God, "Indeed, when I come to the children of Israel and say to them, 'The God of your fathers has sent me to you,' and they say to me, 'What is His name?' what shall I say to them?" And God said to Moses, "I AM WHO I AM." And He said, "Thus you shall say to the children of Israel, 'I AM has sent me to you.'" Exodus 3:11-14

At the burning bush, there is no confusion over what Moses then knew, because God made it abundantly clear. When we find ourselves in moments when God is moving, speaking, or revealing Himself to us—and most likely not with flaming bushes—we need to respond in simple trust and obedience.

After Moses' education in the wilderness, God was ready to move. God would move Moses' heart in such a way that it would move Moses as well. God moves in our hearts the same way today as He speaks to us by His Holy Spirit and by His Holy Word, the Bible. As He speaks to us through His Word,

His Holy Spirit will then lead us to an opportunity to act on what He has shown us. This in no way discounts those periods of waiting, but even during times of waiting, God will open the doors of opportunity when it is time for us to respond—not a moment sooner and never when it is too late.

Removing Life's Blind Spots

God's timing is perfect, and He often waits so we can learn to trust, lean, and rely upon Him alone. Trusting God is an essential aspect of our ongoing relationship with Him, and the longer we walk with Him, the more we should come to trust Him. What does it mean to trust God? Simply put, it is a confidence in God and reliance on Him because of our relationship with Him and who He has been to us. We can look at it this way: by trusting in God, we are saying we rely on the nature and character of God. We rely on His strength and ability to be who He has declared himself to be and to do all He has declared He will do.

When, as Christians, we don't trust God, we are living in contradiction to what we say we believe. Either God is capable, or He isn't. Either God is who He says He is, or He isn't. Either God can do what He says, or He can't. Trusting in God is then expressed in the visible demonstration of acting on that which we believe to be true. We learn through experience as we walk with God, trusting and relying on Him in our lives. It is progressive in nature as well as in our actions. Just look at how your trust in Him increases as you experience His faithfulness in your life.

God continually asks us to trust Him, to take Him at His Word, to place our confidence in His ability, to rely on His Spirit, to obey His commands, to believe His promises, to hand over the reins of our lives to Him, and to let Him steer, because it is here that true blessing is found:

> *Blessed are all those who put their* trust *in Him.* Psalm 2:12 [emphasis added]

Blessed is that man who makes the Lord his trust...
Psalm 40:4 [emphasis added]

Trust *in the Lord, and do good; dwell in the land, and feed on His faithfulness. Delight yourself also in the Lord, and He shall give you the desires of your heart. Commit your way to the Lord,* trust *also in Him, and He shall bring it to pass.* Psalm 37:3-5 [emphasis added]

The temptation for many is to trust in themselves, but the Bible says, *"He who trusts in his own heart is a fool..."* (Proverbs 28:26). Others will trust in wealth, but according Proverbs 11:28, *"He who trusts in his riches will fall . . ."* Still others will trust in power, in strength, in knowledge, in other people, or in the world system. Yet again, we are warned of the danger of such foolish trusting:

"Woe to the rebellious children," says the Lord, "Who take counsel, but not of Me, and who devise plans, but not of My Spirit, that they may add sin to sin; who walk to go down to Egypt, and have not asked My advice, to strengthen themselves in the strength of Pharaoh, and to trust in the shadow of Egypt!" Isaiah 30:1-2

All other trust will fail; only trust in God will prevail.

Moses was trusting in his own strength—not in God—when he killed the Egyptian. How many times do we take matters in our own hands before consulting God? Probably more times than we would like to admit. But hopefully we are learning to trust Him more and depend on His sovereign ability rather than on our limited power.

Moses needed to learn this lesson. Therefore, God allowed him to spend forty years in the desert to learn the dangers and problems associated with trusting in one's own strength. We, too, need to remember this so we don't get ahead of God and act before we pray. If we wait upon God, we will experience victory, or success, in life. We can have a tendency to turn from God at those moments when things go our way and think we are something special, that we made it happen all by ourselves. The temptation is to not recognize God's hand at work or give God the glory for how He worked.

God brings us to places in our walk with Him where we have to make a decision: Are we going to trust God in this situation or not? God may have you in a certain place, season, or trial so you can learn to trust. God may also keep you in that place for as long as it takes you to learn that lesson. Moses needed to stay out in the fields until he got it, until he learned what God was trying to teach him about trust and dependence.

For me, two of the most important verses in the entire Bible are Proverbs 3:5-6: *"Trust in the Lord with all your heart, and lean not on your own understanding; in all your ways acknowledge Him, and He shall direct your paths."* This speaks so simply as to how we are to follow God and discover His will through the process of trusting, waiting, and seeking Him.

As we follow this approach, God, in His time, will show us what steps to take. As we place ourselves in absolute surrender to the Lord's will, as we totally abandon our own natural approach to life, along with our own tendencies and biases, and replace them with a complete and total reliance on and recognition of God's sovereignty, it will result in trusting the all-knowing, all-powerful, ever-present, and eternal God. Such trust will lead you onto His righteous and holy path for your life. Not only does such action honor God, but it is also the blessing that comes with trusting.

U-Haul

In Exodus 3:1-10, we see the Lord appearing and speaking directly to Moses. God comes and calls him to service and gives him his marching orders. Charles Henry Mackintosh, an Irish writer in the mid-1800s, gives us his view on the location to which God leads Moses:

> The "backside of the desert" is where men and things, the world and self, present circumstances and their influences, are all valued at what they are really worth. There it is and there alone, that you will find a Divinely-adjusted balance in which to weigh all within and all around. There are no false colors, no borrowed plumes, no empty pretensions. The enemy of your souls cannot gild the sand of that place. All is reality there. The heart that has found itself in the presence of God at "the backside of the desert" has right thoughts about everything. It is raised far above the exciting influences of this world's schemes. The din and noise, the bustle and confusion of Egypt, do not fall upon the ear in that distant place. The crash in the monetary and commercial world is not heard there; the sigh of ambition is not heard there; this world's fading laurels do not tempt there; the thirst for gold is not felt there; the eye is never dimmed with lust, nor the heart swollen with pride there; human applause does not elate, nor human censure depress there. In a word, everything is set aside save the stillness and light of the Divine presence. God's voice alone is heard, His light enjoyed, His thoughts received. This is the place to which all must go to be educated for the ministry; and there all must remain if they would succeed in the ministry.[7]

Here lies one of the great mysteries of Scripture. God does not need humans to accomplish His plans and purposes. In this case, He could have accomplished His great plan of deliverance for the children of Israel by using His holy, angelic messengers, or He could have appeared to the Israelites personally, or He could have spoken audibly from Heaven—or any number of other divine alternatives. But God chose to use a flawed human agent to accomplish the most sacred of all responsibilities: to be His representative to the people out of love for the people.

Over time, God must have found a better way, right? I mean, this must have been okay for people living in ancient Egypt, but God must have changed how He accomplishes His plans by now. Surely He found a more efficient way to accomplish His holy purposes? Well, that is the mystery. God's most popular strategy for accomplishing His purposes is still to enlist the help of human agents. God loves people, and therefore, God allows us the blessing of being on His team. He doesn't need our help, but He gives us the opportunity to participate, the opportunity to bring other people into a relationship with Him, and the opportunity of leading people out of bondage into freedom, leading them out of the emptiness of this life and into fullness of life in Him.

God loves to work this way. In the same way Moses was to lead the people out of Egypt, so God could lead them into the Promised Land, where they would experience the fullness of His provision, the fullness of His protection, and the fullness of His love and mercy. God has not changed His desire for all who are His, and He wants to do the same for you and me today.

There is a surefire way to find out who your friends are: just tell them you're moving and then ask for their help. The people who show up are generally your true friends. When someone asks you to help them move, something like this usually begins in your mind: *I think I have a dentist appointment,* or *I think my car is getting fixed.* That's right—excuses. We begin to search our minds for anything that might get us off the hook, without lying, of course. No one likes moving. All the packing, the lifting, the loading, the sweating, the unloading, and the unpacking . . . it is backbreaking work. And have you ever noticed it always seems to be 100 degrees outside every time you help someone move? Maybe it just feels that way. The point is that when people ask us to do things we don't want to do, our first response often can be to think of reasons why we can't.

Moses was no different. God wanted help moving, but the difference was that God was going to move an entire nation. We are talking two to three million people. God was going to find out whether Moses was His friend or not. Was Moses up for the backbreaking work of moving a nation? Verse 11 of Exodus 3 begins, *"But Moses...."* You guessed it: Moses began to give his excuses to God.

As the Lord called out to Moses, He said, *"I am the God of your father—the God of Abraham, the God of Isaac, and the God of Jacob"* (Exodus 3:6). Considering this is the first recorded conversation between Moses and God, it makes perfect sense that God would first introduce himself and tell Moses who He is. He is the one and only God, the God of his fathers, the very one who has worked mightily in times past. And He was there to work mightily in a new and powerful way.

This should remind us that God is always looking for men and women He can use. He wants to work in mighty ways. The real question is, are we ready? God has done great things, and He is looking to do great things today. He is seeking those through whom He can work: *"For the eyes of the Lord run to and fro throughout the whole earth, to show Himself strong on behalf of those whose heart is loyal to Him..."* (2 Chronicles 16:9).

D. L. Moody once said, "The world has yet to see what God can do through one man fully committed to Him." Who will be the next person through whom God does a great and mighty work? Are you willing to open yourself up to be used by God in radical ways? Are you willing to be made willing? Are you willing for God to take you totally beyond your abilities and beyond your comfort zone so He may show Himself strong on your behalf? Perhaps you're saying to yourself that you are not qualified, you are not talented enough, you are not worthy, you don't have the proper training, and you are a little scared.

Good! Then you are in a perfect starting place for God to come and fill you up with His power and His ability. As Jesus said to His disciples, *"With men this is impossible, but with God all things are possible"* (Matthew 19:26). Those are the kind of odds that God likes.

When we look at a situation and say, "Man, that is impossible! There is no way we can do that," it is in those types of impossible situations we can see the power of God at work and recognize He is a God who makes a way where there seems to be no way at all.

Listen Closely

As we looked briefly, at the beginning of this chapter, we saw that God likes introductions. We also found that God consistently introduces Himself before He works in a person, and that introduction may take on different shapes. For one person, He may introduce himself as God through a specific answer to prayer. For yet another, He may reveal himself to be the Word of God and may speak directly by bringing clarity to an issue in life or by answering a specific question through His Word.

Ultimately, regardless of the method He uses, God will speak directly to you in a way that is unmistakable, undeniable, and totally God. You will know He is close to you, you will know He sees you, and you will know He hears you. It will be clear He knows and cares for you personally and He is talking to you. It is through that intimate and personal knowledge of who we are that God knows just how to introduce Himself to us. The introduction often takes place at the time we accept Christ as our personal Lord and Savior. It is at this time of a believer's conversion the Lord reveals Himself in such a way that there is no doubting, confusing, or mistaking that He is the one speaking to you.

The Lord has spoken to me repeatedly and, in these moments, has shown me He is there listening to me, watching me, and caring for me. I have often been reading the Bible, and He will speak to me in a very specific way, in a way that is clear and lets me know He knows what is in my heart and on my mind. It is through His Word that He leads me to a Scripture verse or passage that is unequivocally what I have needed at that moment. Perhaps you have had this happen to you. A friend calls "coincidentally" and says something to the effect of, "You know, the Lord has put you on my heart today and I felt I should call you and ask you . . . ?" It is as though God is saying to you and me in these moments, "I am the God of your fathers, the same God who appeared to Abraham, Isaac, and Jacob. I am the great I AM who is speaking to you right now."

What does this have to do with discovering God's will in your life? In order to understand the *what,* it is vital, essential, and fundamental that we begin to learn the *how* of hearing God speak.

God speaks to us through His Word, as we have been learning. It is through His Word that He introduces himself, and it is through His Word that we hear His voice in our lives. The first time you realize God just spoke to you and is calling you out of darkness into His marvelous light, it is fitting to take note of how that happened. That way, you can begin to recognize His voice when He speaks again.

We must never erase from our memories the circumstances surrounding the first time the Lord revealed himself to us, because it may very well be a consistent and repeated way God chooses to reveal Himself to us in the future. What was it that drew you to Him? What was said in that moment? What was the feeling in your heart when you heard His voice? What were you thinking at the time? How did you come to that place where you were asking, knocking, seeking, or searching? What drew you in to listen? What questions did you have? These are all questions you need to consider as you look at the situation from every angle so you can gain as much from it as possible and also receive all God has for you today. Examining those questions may hold the key to many other personal revelations from God.

The Lord has spoken to me many times in the same manner as He did the first time He spoke to me. He knows me best, and He wants to do exceedingly abundantly more than I could ask or even imagine. So it is important that when He speaks, to make it our aim to be listening—listening for His voice and, being an active listener, to be ready to respond when He calls.

10

"I Object!"

⌒♈⌒

But Moses said to God, "Who am I that I should go to Pharaoh, and that I should bring the children of Israel out of Egypt?" Exodus 3:11

Growing up, I loved watching courtroom dramas, whether it was *Perry Mason, Ironside, Matlock, The Practice, L.A. Law,* or many others, I always found them fascinating. In every courtroom scene, inevitably one of the lawyers would stand to his feet and shout, "I object!" They would then give their reason to the judge as to why they were objecting. In some cases, the judge would ask, "On what grounds?"

Well, as Moses began his dialogue with God, he objected to God—never a good thing to do, by the way. Moses would give his reasons to God as to why he didn't feel right for the job God was asking him to perform. That brings us to the first objection.

"Who Am I . . . ?"

"Moses, Moses!" This was the call of God to him from the burning bush. For Moses, this was the beginning of hearing the voice of God. This would begin a long relationship in which he would hear from God and be directed by God to accomplish some amazing things. But as Moses was standing in the presence of God, he no longer felt qualified like he once did forty years earlier. Forty years earlier, Moses thought, *I'm your man, God!* But here we see a different man, a broken man, a humbled man—a man God has shaped perfectly for the work He has prepared. We can learn a lot from Moses and his interaction with God here. We see in God's timing that He has chosen this time and this man. And He says to Moses, *I will send you!*

So Moses responded, *"Who am I . . . ?"* (Exodus 3:11).

Bingo! Moses finally got it! It is not about us, but about God. And we see in Moses' humbled response that he was no longer depending on his abilities, but on God's. We see he recognizes there is emptiness to be found in man's ability, foolishness to be found in man's wisdom, and weakness in man's strength. As the Apostle Paul pointed out, *"The foolishness of God is wiser than men, and the weakness of God is stronger than men"* (1 Corinthians 1:25). This is also important for us to understand, but we, too, often miss it, overlook it, or simply dismiss it. Man continually tries to do the work of God out of his own wealth, wisdom, and strength, but it isn't until man sees the futility of a work done apart from God that God is able to say, *"Come now, therefore, and I will send you . . ."* (Exodus 3:10).

Egypt was the leading nation of the ancient world. It was militarily unmatched, educationally unparalleled, and economically unequaled. But with all their wisdom, knowledge, and resources, nothing would be able to stop what God was about to do next.

I am totally convinced that when God brings us to the place where we say, "Who am I? I can't do this . . . I am not worthy . . . I don't have the resources to accomplish this thing . . . without you, God, I am unable," this is when God can work. When we move out of the way and allow God to have His way, He looks at the situation and says, "Now I can work. Now you are ready," because it is then—and only then—there will be no mistaking it was done by the very hand of God, not the hand of man. There will be no mistaking it was done by God—and God alone.

We must all be brought to the same place Moses was: not necessarily a Mount Horeb, but to a greater mountain, the one within our own hearts. We must be brought to the place where we recognize if God is not with us, if God is not moving us, if God is not in what we are doing, we don't want to be a part of it or anything from within ourselves, because our efforts will not succeed. When you are at your Mount Horeb, be prepared to hear the voice of God calling your name. Be ready to receive a mission that you will look at and think *I can't do this!* That is God's divine tipping point. It is when you can see God's hand move where you can't, but where He can.

God, of course, saw Moses' doubt and fear, and in this place, He sought to encourage His servant by giving him a sign: *"And this shall be a sign to you that I have sent you: When you have brought the people out of Egypt, you shall serve God on this mountain"* (Exodus 3:12). A sign is good. Moses probably thought *Okay, now we are talking! A sign would be helpful! God, thanks! Okay, what kind of sign? Hmmm. Let me think. Maybe rain in the desert? Perhaps making the moon disappear? Maybe transporting me into Heaven for a quick visit?* No, the sign God gave to Moses would be that after he led the people out of Egypt, he would come back to that mountain, where he would serve God.

What? Are you kidding? How is that a sign? How does that show me that You will be with me, and how does that show me that You will do this work? Ah, that's the point. And what is the point? Faith. The importance of this sign is found in the fact that the sign could be confirmed only *after* Moses went. The confirmation to Moses was based on his step of faith to go and take God at His Word.

Moses was looking at the problems that lay ahead, while God was making promises for the future. God was going to show himself strong through Moses, but Moses needed to respond in faith if he wanted to see God deliver. Moses' faith and God's faithfulness were to work together in total harmony to accomplish God's plan of deliverance. God was seeking faith from Moses, and if we fast-forward to Hebrews 11, we will see Moses' faith shined and sparkled like a diamond in the sun. His actions say to us that if we will just step out in faith, trust in the promises of God, and look to God alone, then we, too, will see all that God can do through and on behalf of a vessel willing to walk by faith and not by sight.

God is looking for the same faith in us today that He was drawing out in Moses. He places us in situations where He tests our faith to see if it is genuine. Maybe there are promises from Scripture that God has shown you, and He is asking you to step out in faith and trust Him. Perhaps God has revealed a promise that is specific for you, and the thing that stands in the way of its coming to pass is your faith to step out, to go out, to act upon it, or to let go.

I believe God would say a similar thing to you and me as He said to Moses: our stepping out in faith is what will activate His promises coming true in our lives. God will work to complete His promises as we trust Him to complete them. That is good news! We don't have to go it alone. God will be there to support, guide, direct, and protect His chosen servants as we are walking in His will. The Lord declares, *"I will certainly be with you."*

"Who Is Sending Me?"

Knowing and determining it is God who is calling you to do a specific work is very important and should be surrounded in prayer. Once you know God is the one calling you, don't hesitate. Don't dwell on your inadequacies; we all have them. When God calls you, He will equip you to do the very work He has called you to do: *"Now may the God of peace who brought up our Lord Jesus from the dead, that great Shepherd of the sheep, through the blood of the everlasting covenant, make you complete in every good work to do His will . . . "* (Hebrews 13:20-21).

Moses doesn't do this. Instead, he continues his cross-examination of God as he is overwhelmed by the massive mission placed before him. Moses is feeling inadequate and insecure. Many of us have felt that, too. I know I have. A feeling of inadequacy in a God-sized task is normal, and it is in this moment Moses asks a question for which *he* needs an answer. Moses asked the question because he needed more reassurance. When Moses went to the children of Israel, they never asked Moses for the name of God. It seems this was all Moses, again needing some personal reassurances. Moses, in so many words, asks the question, "What is Your name?" (see Exodus 3:13).

God is very gracious. He knows our weaknesses, yet He is still willing to meet us where we are so we are able to move on to the next step. God had already identified Himself back in verse 6, but Moses needed more information. I have heard it suggested that God was upset with Moses for asking this question, so instead of giving him His name, He basically said, "Look, Moses, I am who I am. That ought to be good enough for you."

Certainly the name I AM brings up its own set of questions, but I don't think this was God's way of rebuking Moses. It seems to me to be just the opposite. God's seemingly cryptic yet simple phrase, "I AM WHO I AM," contains within it more about God's nature and character than we can ever fully understand this side of Heaven. We could spend eternity looking at what the name of God reveals to us, but for the purposes of our study, we will look at one key aspect of what His name meant for Moses, and also what it means for us today.

In essence, what God is saying as He declares Himself to be the great I AM, is that He is the one who is, who was, and who always will be. You see, contained within the name I AM is the total sufficiency of God and the utter completeness of God. He is Creator and Sustainer; He is ALL. God is promising, through His name, to be Moses' all in all.

Whatever Moses would need, God would be. When Moses needed a miracle, God would be his miracle. When Moses needed bread, God would be bread. When Moses needed water, God would be water. When Moses needed direction, God would be the cloud by day and the pillar of fire by night. Whatever Moses needed to accomplish the task ahead of him, God would meet that need, because He is the I AM.

God will be only those things that are consistent with His nature, with His Word, and with that which will bring Him glory. One such example would be in the provision of manna (see Exodus 16) given to the children of Israel in the desert. God gives them no more and no less than what they need, when they need it. For *where God guides, God provides*. The first time I heard this phrase was from Chuck Smith, senior pastor of Calvary Chapel Costa Mesa. To this day, it is the best and most concise way to speak of the combined work of God's direction and provision.

These first two questions raised by Moses, "Who am I?" and "Who is sending me?" contain within them two fundamentals in discovering God's will for your life. John Calvin summarized it perfectly at the beginning of his famous writing, *Institutes of the Christian Religion*, by saying, "Nearly all the wisdom we possess, that is to say, true and sound wisdom, consists of two parts: the knowledge of God and of ourselves."[8] God used Moses' questions to teach him about both.

"They Won't Believe Me."

Have you ever been afraid of what people might think of you? I would suspect we all have at some point in our lives. It may have been during that awkward, overly self-conscious period in junior high school, where popularity and acceptance from our peers meant everything to us. Or perhaps it stems from those times when we had to give a speech in front of a group of people and could feel all eyes in the room were on us. With our palms getting sweatier by the minute, we were worried about making fools of ourselves. Perhaps it was that first job interview, or maybe it was when you were trying to make a good impression on your future spouse. Whether you share some of these experiences or have others of your own, we all have been concerned at one time or another about what others may think about us.

Even as Christians, we can be assaulted with the fear of how others perceive us. These fears are not justified in God's social economy. If we fall prey to the god of perception, image, and acceptance, it only will serve to handicap us. If we abide in such a place, we will not live in the fullness of what God has intended for us.

Adam and Eve lived in paradise and had a fellowship with God that was so rich and full it is hard for us to even imagine. Their fellowship with God was so perfect it is difficult for us to see why they would do anything to hinder that relationship, but they made choices that resulted in restricting the fullness of God in their lives.

We can do the same. We limit the fullness of God's blessing in our lives when we allow ourselves to be swayed by fear. Many people are crippled by fear. Unfortunately, allowing fear to keep you frozen really only leads to your hurting yourself. Think of all the people with a fear of flying—pteromerhanophobia, as it is called—and all they miss out on. Think of all the beautiful places they will never see due to this fear. Yet 2 Timothy 1:7 tells us,

"For God has not given us a spirit of fear, but of power and of love and of a sound mind."

Moses was certainly afraid of how he would be perceived by his fellow comrades, and he wondered if they would even receive him and God's message of deliverance. Moses was so fearful it nearly prevented him from entering into the joy of the Lord's service and all the blessings that come with being used by God. God had a Promised Land flowing with milk and honey awaiting Moses and the children of Israel, but Moses seemed content to stay in the desert.

Today we, too, can miss out on God's best. We can forfeit much of what God has for us simply because of our fear of failure. We can get so comfortable and set in our ways that we are unwilling to change. We can be unyielding to change, even when it means those circumstances in which we live are not good or healthy for us, simply because the fear of change prevents us from making that first step. Jesus said in John 10:10, *"I have come that they may have life, and that they may have it more abundantly."* We miss out on this abundant life when we let fear keep us from serving God and following His plan for our lives. What we need is more faith and less fear. As 1 John 5:4 tells us, *"For whatever is born of God overcomes the world. And this is the victory that has overcome the world—our faith."* By faith we can overcome not only fear, but also the downward pull of this world. Faith in Christ raises us up in victory.

The companions of fear are doubt and discouragement. These two evil twins are always walking hand in hand, looking for new ways to befriend the Christian. These two companions are not friends of ours, but weapons the enemy likes to use to cripple the life of a believer. Giving into fear, doubt, and discouragement will keep you on the sidelines. Or worse yet, they can take you out of the race. These are such effective weapons that Satan used them against Jesus himself. Satan asked Jesus several times, *"If You are the son of God . . ."* trying to bring doubt into the equation and thereby getting Jesus to give into the temptation (see Matthew 4:3, 6).

Moses was also in the desert, much like Jesus, and Satan was hoping that Moses' doubts would get the best of him. So far, his tactics were working, as Moses doubted his ability to accomplish this mission God had for him. Moses decided to ask God for further confirmation.

As the Lord leads us, we often seek further confirmation. We want to know that we clearly heard from God and that it wasn't just our imaginations. We want to know God is the one doing the leading, guiding, and speaking, and that all other influences, motives, desires, or emotions are not influencing our decision. It is one thing to be genuinely seeking direction and answers to God's leading, but it is quite another to simply offer up questions in an attempt to get out of what you are being asked to do.

God is patient beyond measure and has a limitless love for His children. So instead of getting mad at Moses for his wavering, doubting, and delaying, God continued to help Moses through his indecision. Jesus also took time to help Thomas with his personal doubts (see John 20:24-29). Here in Exodus 3-4, God was speaking directly to Moses. It has been my experience that God often will speak to me directly through His Word, giving me a specific verse or passage I need, the one that perfectly addresses the very issue I am struggling with. This is all part of what the Word of God will do for every believer. As the Apostle Paul pointed out in 2 Timothy 3:16-17: "*All Scripture is given by inspiration of God, and is profitable for doctrine, for reproof, for correction, for instruction in righteousness, that the man of God may be complete, thoroughly equipped for every good work.*"

"I Am Not Gifted."

Then Moses said to the Lord, "O my Lord, I am not eloquent, neither before nor since You have spoken to Your servant; but I am slow of speech and slow of tongue." Exodus 4:10

I'm not qualified. I'm not trained. I don't have the experience. And the "I . . . " excuses kept coming! The issue for Moses here, and for us, is not whether I am *able*, but am I *willing?* And, is the I AM calling me? God is more interested in our availability than our ability. When we focus on our inabilities or our weaknesses, we place the emphasis on ourselves and take the focus off God. The real source of power is God, not us. God is the one who will do the work. God is greater than any of our weaknesses. God is the one who will supply us with all we need to fulfill his call in our lives: *"For it is God who works in you both to will and to do for His good pleasure"* (Philippians 2:13). When it comes to the call of God on our lives, we always must be aware that it is, first and foremost, *all* God working through us. Within the call God has given us, He will give us the means to accomplish all that is needed to answer that call—for His will, for His way, by His power, and for His glory.

Moses' excuses were beginning to border on disobedience at this point. God had already given him reassurance after reassurance, yet Moses refused to simply obey. Amazingly, God didn't turn Moses into a pile of dirt, but instead God said, *"Who has made man's mouth? Or who makes the mute, the deaf, the seeing, or the blind? Have not I, the Lord? Now therefore, go, and I will be with your mouth and teach you what you shall say"* (Exodus 4:11-12). A rough translation in today's vernacular would be, "Hey, Moses, I am God. I made you. I made your mouth. And if I can make you and your mouth, then I can surely put in your mouth the words I want you to say. Now, stop your complaining, stop delaying, and get moving. I will provide you what you need to say when you need to say it."

We have a similar promise today: *"Now when they bring you to the synagogues and magistrates and authorities, do not worry about how or what you should answer, or what you should say. For the Holy Spirit will teach you in that very hour what you ought to say"* (Luke 12:11-12).

Today God has given His Holy Spirit to every believer to guide us and give us His words to speak. I had a very real and personal experience with this principle a few years ago. I was asked to do a funeral for a member of our church. The funeral was going to be held at a different church in another town, which was closer for more people who would be attending. This was a mega church, with around 18,000 members. So I was thinking *Okay, God, is this funeral going to be packed-out in this huge facility? Is the senior pastor of this mega church (whom I admire and respect but have never met) going to be there?* I was a little nervous.

When I got to the church that day for the service, I met with the family and found a quiet place to look over my notes one final time. The service started and the sanctuary was about half full. There was no sign of the pastor, but I still thought, *Who knows? Maybe he'll still pop in.* I began the service with prayer and said a few opening remarks. Then I turned things over to the family, who had a video they wanted to show, followed by several family members who would speak. Then the service would return to me to deliver the funeral message.

During this time, a very interesting thing happened. The Lord stirred my heart and spoke to me in such a way that I sensed He was saying, "Put your notes away. I want you to say something else."

To which I said, "What? Oh, you have got to be kidding me! There are hundreds of people here, and I can't just abandon my message. This is a funeral. I don't want to ruin this very important time for family and friends as they remember this man. I ... I ... I ... " And so went the conversation between me and God in my heart and mind.

Finally, I said, "Okay, Lord. If You want to say something different than what I have prepared, then You need to give it to me, because I have absolutely no time to develop a new message." Just then, I believe the Lord saw a mustard seed of faith in me, and He gave me a Scripture verse. So I found the verse in my Bible and read it.

Then I said, yet again, "Are you sure this is the verse you want me to use for the funeral? It doesn't seem to fit."

The answer: "Yes, just trust Me."

"Okay, Lord."

Just about then I could see the last family member was almost finished speaking. When I got up, I brought my notes with me, but I told everyone I felt the Lord had just spoken to me, and I wasn't supposed to use the message I had prepared. So I placed the notes on the stage behind me, opened my Bible, and began to read what the Lord had given me. The next thing I knew, twenty minutes had gone by. I had referenced about eight other passages, and I was now asking people to give their lives to Christ. Fifteen people accepted Christ that morning. After witnessing God at work in that way, I was able to see why God wanted me to trust Him.

God knew who was there that day. He knew what those people needed to hear to be brought into a relationship with Him, and it wasn't what I had prepared. What a joy and a blessing it was to hear the Lord speak, to respond, and to see His mighty hand do an incredible work of salvation. All the glory belongs to God, because it was God who did all the work. But God put up with my questions, because He knew I needed to work through my ability to have faith.

What would have happened if I didn't listen? What if I didn't trust? What if I had let fear stop me from obeying God's leading? I would have missed out on an opportunity to be used by God, and those people would have left without hearing what God wanted them to hear that day. Now, I believe at some point God would have given them the message they needed to hear, but it wouldn't have been by me, and it might not have been on that day.

We rob ourselves of so much when we decide not to heed His voice and His leading. We can be delaying the work God wants to do in and through us and we can rob others of the blessings God wants to give them at that moment.

God was speaking to Moses and asking Him to have faith in Him and in His ability to do what He said He would do for Moses. Yet all this doesn't seem to be enough for Moses, and as a result, Moses is in real danger. Any time we continue to question God in light of His repeated direction to us, we tread on dangerous ground. For as we see with Moses, what was borderline disobedience now seemed to be the final straw, and God began to get angry at Moses: *So the anger of the Lord was kindled against Moses . . .* (Exodus 4:14).

I am not sure about you, but believe me, the last place I want to be is in the presence of God, trying His patience. When Jacob wrestled with God (see Genesis 32:22-32), the result was a dislocated hip and a lifelong limp. There are consequences when we set ourselves against God and His plan for our lives. Whether we wrestle with God or simply lack the faith to do as He is directing us, we only hurt ourselves.

Moses' lack of faith in God not only kindled God's anger, but the result was he missed God's blessing. God again was patient and kind and knew Moses would eventually do the right thing, but because Moses was being obstinate and refusing to speak for God, his brother Aaron was chosen for that assignment. Moses was missing out on God's best for his life.

It is always good to share the responsibility in ministry. We are many members in one Body of Christ, so everyone has a part to play (see Romans 12:4-8). However, when God has called you to do something, and you give that task to someone else, you rob yourself of the joy and blessing of doing what God wanted *you* to do. You are robbed of the blessings—and also the rewards that are to come.

God's goodness and grace do not stop with the gift of salvation. He continues to give good gifts to His children. He desires to reward all who serve Him faithfully. Just listen to God's heart:

> *If anyone's work which he has built on it endures, he will receive a reward.* 1 Corinthians 3:14

> *Let no one cheat you of your reward . . .* Colossians 2:18

> *And whatever you do, do it heartily, as to the Lord and not to men, knowing that from the Lord you will receive the reward of the inheritance; for you serve the Lord Christ.* Colossians 3:23-24

The Final Forty

Moses finally decided to trust God. No more excuses, no more delays, it was time to follow God's leading. Of course, there is much we can learn as we follow Moses during the many years of wilderness wandering but, simply put, from this point forward we see that as Moses submitted his will to God's plan, there was blessing. But when Moses acted outside of God's will, taking things into his own hands, difficulty, rebuke, and hardship followed.

As we follow God, we will face the same cycle. We will face consequences when we blow it, when we take control of things, and when we disobey God. It is important to remember that in the midst of all the difficult times we are sure to face because of our flesh and our failures, the Lord is with us. We must remember it is God who is on our side, and it is God who has promised He will never leave us or forsake us (see Hebrews 13:5). We are God's children, and He can work everything—even our mistakes—for good: *"And we know that all things work together for good to those who love God, to those who are the called according to His purpose. For whom He foreknew, He also predestined to be conformed to the image of His Son . . ."* (Romans 8:28-29). As we learn to follow and obey His Word, as we listen to His voice, we will grow in the knowledge, understanding, and wisdom of God.

The life of Moses is an example to us all. It shows us a man who gave himself to the work and ministry to which God had called him. Moses was a man whom the Lord used in mighty and powerful ways. He was also a man whom God spoke to and through. He was a man who is referenced nearly eighty times in the New Testament. He was a man who had a rough start and who almost missed out on the opportunity of a lifetime due to doubt and fear. He was a man who was not perfect, who did great things and stupid things, and for this reason and a few more, he is a man to whom many can relate. We all make mistakes, but we need to be encouraged that just as God worked through this man, mistakes and all, God can work and will work through us—if we are yielded, trust, obey, and have faith the size of a mustard seed.

Final Thoughts

We need to take time to listen to God. Then we must take time to respond to God. When God stirs our hearts, we need to act upon that stirring. The stirring God does within our hearts should result in our putting faith into action.

It is okay to ask God questions about what He is showing us. Any honest and prayerful seeking of God will result in His answering. Jesus said, *"Ask, and it will be given to you; seek, and you will find; knock, and it will be opened to you"* (Matthew 7:7). However, we must be careful not to use those questions as excuses not to serve.

Moses needed to be willing, just as we do, to let go of cultural methods to accomplish God's ministry. As the Apostle Paul pointed out, *"For the wisdom of this world is foolishness with God"* (1 Corinthians 3:19). It isn't about business plans. It isn't about strategizing with the latest trends in an area. Moses had to learn that service wasn't about what is the most efficient way to cross the Nile. It isn't about how to feed millions of people in the desert with nothing. It had to be God's will, God's way, and for God's glory.

We need to remember we can't accomplish anything apart from Christ. All too often, we think we know what God wants to do, and we go full steam ahead. Moses' life should teach us not to be impulsive and presumptuous, but instead to wait on God and let Him come to us and show us the way.

PART THREE

❦

Where the Rubber
Meets the Road

11

Power
FOR THE
Journey

✑

You shall receive power . . . Acts 1:8

There is a great story about Alfred Nobel, the inventor of dynamite. One morning when he woke up and began to read the morning newspaper, he came across the obituaries where, to his amazement, he was reading his own death announcement. What was a simple case of mistaken identity became a moment of awakening for Alfred Nobel. As he read the summary of his life, he was surprised at the name given him: the Dynamite King. "Was this how the world saw me?" he thought. "Is this the legacy I am to leave, a man who made millions from creating explosives, a merchant of death?" All the other pursuits of his life and humanitarian efforts were not mentioned.

Nobel was horrified and humiliated that this was how he would be remembered. It was at this moment he set out to make clear to the world the true meaning and purpose of his life. He decided to use the fortune he made in dynamite for five annual prizes to be given to those who made outstanding contributions in physics, chemistry, physiology or medicine, literature, and peace (a sixth category of economics was added later). Now, most people who have heard of Alfred Nobel are completely unaware that he was the Dynamite King. Rather, they know him as the one who created the Nobel Peace Prize.

As we turn our attention to the New Testament and to the Holy Spirit, you could call the Holy Spirit the true Dynamite King, as He is about to burst on the scene in the Book of Acts with flaming tongues of fire and lead the church into a dynamic new era. In the Book of Acts, we see God move in mighty ways to accomplish *exceedingly abundantly* above all man could think, ask, or even imagine (see Ephesians 3:20). And God accomplished all this through ordinary men and women who were yielded and surrendered to Him. They were men and women who sought to live godly lives by offering themselves completely to Him, allowing the Holy Spirit free reign to move in them to accomplish His will, plans, and purposes.

The power and work of the Holy Spirit is not new; the Holy Spirit worked in times past in mighty and powerful ways. However, when we come to the Book of Acts, we see the Holy Spirit branching out. Prior to this point and the outpouring of the Holy Spirit in the New Testament, the Holy Spirit only came upon select individuals.

Such was the case that we see in the life of David, Saul, Joshua, and others. But this *coming upon* of the Holy Spirit was both selective and temporary. When a person puts his or her faith and trust in Jesus today, the Word of God promises the Holy Spirit will take up permanent residence within that new believer. Paul referred to this as our *guarantee* in Ephesians 1:14.

So when it comes to following God, the Holy Spirit holds a significant role in leading a believer: *"For as many as are led by the Spirit of God, these are sons of God"* (Romans 8:14). Certainly there are many different aspects of the Holy Spirit, as well as many different functions of the Holy Spirit. But we want consider how the power of the Holy Spirit leads and assists believers in following God and determining His will for their lives.

Famous Last Words

A person's final words can say a lot about what is important to them. For example, Napoleon cried out, "Josephine!" on May 5, 1821 before he breathed his last breath.

P.T. Barnum's final words in 1891 were, "How were the receipts today at Madison Square Garden?"

Former President Grover Cleveland's last words were, "I have tried so hard to do right."

And before Jesus ascended into Heaven, His final words to His disciples would reveal the next step in the will of God for their lives: *"But you shall receive power when the Holy Spirit has come upon you; and you shall be witnesses to Me in Jerusalem, and in all Judea and Samaria, and to the end of the earth"* (Acts 1:8).

Oftentimes when we think of the apostles, we consider them to be superhuman, in the same category as a superhero. We believe they were able to leap tall buildings in a single bound, run faster than a speeding bullet, and were more powerful than a locomotive. Although these men did posses some unique, supernatural abilities, none of those gifts came from them or were a result of their own efforts. They were given to them by God.

These men whom God chose were just ordinary men God used to do extraordinary things for His glory, honor, and praise. Their mission to glorify God and point others to Him is the same as ours is today: *you shall be witnesses to Me . . .*

God never changes. Hebrews 13:8 declares: *"Jesus Christ is the same yesterday, today, and forever."* And because God never changes, I believe the mission for the Church today remains unchanged. This means God's will for the apostles is also God's will for His people. The same marching orders He gave the apostles yesterday is the same one He gives to us today, and it forever remains the call of every disciple following after Jesus Christ. This is a call to all men and women of God, regardless of who they are or what they may do for a living.

If you are a follower of Jesus, then you are a living testimony and witness for Jesus. This means that if you are a mom, you are a witness to your children, telling them about Jesus as you raise them. You are a witness to their teachers in their schools, among other parents on the playground, in your home, and in your neighborhood.

If you are in the workplace, you are a witness of Jesus in how you work, in your interaction with your coworkers, and in honoring your boss and employer as you serve them as unto Jesus.

If you are married, you are a witness of Jesus in how you love your spouse and build your Christ-centered life and marriage.

Your witness is given in words to those around you, and your living example is a reflection of what is important to you in a wondering, wanting, and watching world in desperate need of the life-saving, life-giving, and living power of Jesus.

Jesus spoke these final words in Acts 1:8 just before He ascended into Heaven. It was a triumphant moment as the Church age was about to be ushered into a new era and a new way of relating to God through the indwelling of His Spirit. It was a new mission and commission. In these final words of Christ, we have the primary job for the Church in the world today. And because we, as individuals, form the Church of Jesus Christ, this means it is with this statement that we see the beginning of the Church's existence.

As we read these words of Jesus, we see and hear an important aspect of God's will being revealed to all who will follow Jesus Christ. Now that we have identified a major part of God's perfect will for our lives, it is important that we take a moment to look at the two main categories that make up the application of God's will in our lives.

God's General Will

The first category of God's will is His *general* will. God's general will is easy for us to determine, because it is clearly spelled out in God's Word. There are many commands God has given to us, commands His Word plainly lists out, which means there are many aspects of God's will that should not be mysterious or hard to determine.

For example, the greatest commandant of God tells us to love the Lord our God with all our heart, soul, strength, and mind, and to love others as ourselves (see Luke 10:27). If we are living in and under this commandment and the will of God for our lives, then we will be able to love as God calls us to love. Practically, we know God's Word tells us not to steal, so if you are faced with the temptation to take something that does not belong to you, the will of God in this situation isn't a mystery. Don't steal. Out of love for God and for others, you should not want to steal.

God's general will is the same for all people at all times. There is no mystery about it. So just do it! His general will is clearly revealed to us in the Bible, so the only issue is one of obedience, not discernment. The question then becomes whether we are going to do what His Word tells us to do. Will we obey? It doesn't require a degree in theology, we don't have to pray and ask for wisdom, and we don't need to cry out, "Lord, what is Your will for me in this situation?" It is simply a matter of either taking God at His Word, and, out of love for Him, obeying. We obey and do not steal, or we disobey and do steal.

Equally, God never will reveal anything to us that cannot first be found in His Word. So with regard to God's general will, it is less about discovering or discerning it and more about obeying it. And because our God is a God of order, He never will ask us to do anything outside of His order.

Much of God's will falls into this category. Living as God has called us to live is largely living in His order of love and acting in obedience to the already revealed commands found in the Word of God. I believe if we simply did what we already know the Bible tells us to do, it would eliminate much of the confusion we encounter in seeking His will.

God's Specific Will

On the other hand, we find the second category of God's will: His *specific* will. Determining God's specific will can be more difficult and even nerve-racking at times, but God promises to be our peace. Whenever we step out in faith, none of us can say that we always have 100 percent surety when it comes to knowing God's will. There will be times when you do have the *peace . . . which surpasses all understanding . . .* (Philippians 4:7), and you will have His Word that allows you to have complete confidence as you step out toward what the Lord is leading you to do.

But there will be other times when we are not 100 percent sure, or times when we will make mistakes and misinterpret the application of God's Word in our own life. But we do have the assurance from God that even if we do make a mistake and don't get it 100 percent right, God can and will use even our mistakes for good and to work in all to accomplish His perfect will in our lives. We have this promise from Romans 8:27-28: *"Now He who searches the hearts knows what the mind of the Spirit is, because He makes intercession for the saints according to the will of God. And we know that all things work together for good to those who love God, to those who are the called according to His purpose."*

Of course, these verses are not an excuse to make decisions without fully seeking God or waiting on Him for direction. We don't go into decisions halfheartedly thinking *Oh, well, if this isn't the right decision, no biggie. God will fix it and work it all out for good.* God can and does work all things for good and for His perfect will, and it is in this place that we see the depth of His measureless grace and mercy. However, if we do so flippantly, we tread upon the fine line of abusing the grace of God.

Just because God is full of mercy and grace does not lessen our responsibility as followers of Jesus to be as fully convinced as possible of His will before we step out. Nor does it diminish God's law of reaping and sowing in our lives. Even though God is gracious and merciful to work things for our good, wrong decisions still have consequences and can cause unnecessary heartache, hardship, and even hurt to others. And some of those consequences are lifelong. We need to be diligent to do all we can to ensure we are listening to God before we act and that we check it against what He has already said. It is only after you feel you have as clear a direction as possible from God that you should step out in faith.

What kind of help does the Helper give? How can we walk in the same power the apostles walked in?

Not the Magic 8-Ball

Do you remember the Magic 8-Ball? Developed in 1950, this plastic ball looked like an oversized, billiard ball and was designed to be a toy fortune-telling device that contained a series of twenty different answer combinations for questions you might ask. For example, you might ask a question like, "Will Sally say yes if I ask her to the prom?"

You would then shake the Magic 8-Ball and await its answer, which might be, "Don't count on it," or "Outlook not so good." Bummer! But the thing about the Magic 8-Ball was that if you didn't get the answer you wanted, you could just keep shaking it until the answer you were hoping for came to the surface.

The Holy Spirit is not like the Magic 8-Ball. He is not some sort of fortune-telling novelty item. The Holy Spirit is the third person of the Holy Trinity of God. We need to be careful not to make Him anything less than God or to diminish the role He plays in leading people to Christ and leading the believer in following Christ.

The Trinity consists of the Father, Son, and the Holy Spirit. They all are God—united but unique, and equal but distinctly different in function. One function of the Holy Spirit is to help guide us as believers, to lead us, and to give us understanding and wisdom so we can walk in accordance with the will, plans, and purposes of God.

Where confusion often comes into the life of a believer is during those times of trying to determine how the Spirit actually leads, and seeking to discern what is from the Spirit of God and what is from the flesh of man. In order to discern what is from the Spirit of God and not from today's culture or your own selfish desires, you must rely on the Word of God, the Bible.

The Spirit of God leads by speaking from Scripture: *"However, when He, the Spirit of truth, has come, He will guide you into all truth; for He will not speak on His own authority, but whatever He hears He will speak; and He will tell you things to come. He will glorify Me, for He will take of what is Mine and declare it to you"* (John16:13-14). The only source of truth is God's Word. Jesus prayed, *"Sanctify them by Your truth. Your word is truth"* (John 17:17). You cannot be led by God and by His Spirit apart from God's Word.

God's First Words to the First Man

Ever since God created man, He has spoken to man. In the beginning when God created man and placed him in the center of this brand new paradise on Earth, the Garden of Eden, the Word of God came to him.

What were the first words spoken from God to man? Did God speak of all the mysteries of the universe? Did He speak of His greatness and power? Did He give man a guided tour of the planet, explaining how everything works? Sometimes we can learn as much about someone by what isn't said as by what is said.

There is much that God could have communicated to Adam as He broke the heavenly silence to speak to him, but God kept it simple and gave Adam instructions on how to live a God-honoring and God-glorifying life, a life that would bring man joy and fulfillment. God spoke simple and clear instructions, which, if they had been followed by Adam, would have kept him in the center of this beautiful paradise on Earth and would also have kept him in the center of God's perfect will.

It is hard to imagine the beauty, purity, and freedom in the Garden at that moment for Adam. It was perfection, beauty, and freedom in its purest form, the likes of which humanity has never experienced since then. But one day, we will see and experience it again when God creates a new Heaven and a new Earth. Until then we can only imagine the setting. It is from the splendor of this scene that God spoke to Adam: *"And the Lord God commanded the man, saying, 'Of every tree of the garden you may freely eat; but of the tree of the knowledge of good and evil you shall not eat, for in the day that you eat of it you shall surely die'"* (Genesis 2:16-17).

You have probably heard the expression, "You don't get a second chance to make a first impression." Well, this is not only God's first impression with the world's first man, but it is also our first look at the type of relationship God is establishing between Himself and mankind. When God spoke to Adam for the first time, He not only communicated a tremendous amount of information in just one sentence, but God also gave us insight into discovering His will for our lives. As God spoke to Adam, He made it clear to Adam (and to us) that any and all relationship with God is to be based on God's Word to man. As God spoke to Adam, He gave Adam a promise. Adam was free to enjoy this paradise and all God had placed in it, but there was one prohibition: Do not eat from the Tree of the Knowledge of Good and Evil.

God has given us many great and wonderful promises and freedoms to enjoy, but there are also prohibitions He has spoken to us through His Word, prohibitions that are not meant to restrict us as much as they are meant to protect us. The question for us, then, becomes the same question Adam was faced with: What are we going to do with the Word of God? God has revealed His perfect will for man in His Word, and what we do with God's Word is *everything.*

When God spoke to Adam, He spoke in a command—not because He was power hungry or because He was a dictatorial king wanting to rule over man with an iron fist, but because He wanted to establish His divine authority and see how man would respond to that authority.

God has given us the choice to obey His Word or to not obey His Word, to submit to His divine authority revealed through the Word or to not submit to His divine authority. It is crucial that we not only *see* Him as Lord of our lives, but that we also *surrender* to Him as Lord over our lives. Submission is an ongoing issue in the lives of all who follow Christ; it doesn't go away once we become Christians.

Jesus reminds us of this relentless battle against our wills: *"Then He said to them all, 'If anyone desires to come after Me, let him deny himself, and take up his cross daily, and follow Me. For whoever desires to save his life will lose it, but whoever loses his life for My sake will save it'"* (Luke 9:23-24). Submission is not partial, not occasional, and not sporadic; submission must be full, complete, all the time, and in all areas of our lives.

Will we submit to His Word? Will we allow God to direct our steps? He is the one in charge. As we seek to follow God, we must remember that submission is where this relationship begins, and it is so often where this relationship begins to go wrong. Our lives are not our own. God is our Creator, Sustainer, Provider, Healer, Helper, Comforter, Redeemer, and so much more. Therefore, He possesses all rights to our lives and all authority over our lives. We get into trouble when we want to do things our way and not God's way. God spoke to Adam, and he had a choice to make: Would he follow God's Word or not?

There is no greater, single component to our success or failure in following God than in our devotion—or lack of devotion—to the Word of God. It is impossible to follow God apart from following His Word. It is impossible to be in the center of God's will and not have God's Word in the center of your life. God has spoken to us, and we have a choice to make: Will we follow God's Word or not?

This is one place where the Helper, the Holy Spirit, assists the believer. The Holy Spirit uses the Word of God to help the child of God stay in the will of God. One way the Spirit uses the Word of God to help the believer is by strengthening the believer. As the Apostle Paul prayed for the Ephesian believers, *"That He would grant you, according to the riches of His glory, to be strengthened with might through His Spirit..."* (Ephesians 3:16).

Let me illustrate it this way. When you eat food, your body takes in the food and digests it, then converts it into energy, thereby giving your physical body the strength it needs to function. When we read and mediate on the Word of God, it is food for your soul, and the Holy Spirit takes that food in and digests it, converting it into spiritual energy, thereby giving you the spiritual strength to function and live the life that God calls you to live.

What we find, all too often, are Christians who are spiritually malnourished. Just as physical malnourishment can cause pain, weakness, confusion, and even blindness, spiritual malnourishment can cause pain in the Body of Christ. It can cause Christians who are weak in their walk to become confused and unable to discern what is right, and it can even lead to spiritual blindness. We must stop feasting on the things of the world, because all the world offers us, sells us, and shows us is only junk food for the soul. The cure for spiritual malnutrition is a consistent and well-balanced diet of the Word of God. This allows the Holy Spirit to strengthen the believer.

The Right Mindset

Next, living in the center of God's will means pursuing and producing the Fruit of the Spirit. Jesus said, *"By this My Father is glorified, that you bear much fruit..."* (John 15:8). Simply put, bearing the Fruit of the Spirit glorifies God. If we are producing the Fruit of the Spirit in our lives, we are bringing glory to God, and we are living in the center of His will.

So the question becomes, what does the Fruit of the Spirit look like? Galatians 5 gives us the most complete, single listing of the Fruit of the Spirit, in verses 22-23: *"But the fruit of the Spirit is love, joy, peace, longsuffering, kindness, goodness, faithfulness, gentleness, self-control..."* As believers in Christ, we are given the presence of the Holy Spirit to dwell within us and to produce through us the Fruit of the Spirit. But in order for our lives to be marked by the quantity and quality of fruitfulness that God desires, we must both cooperate with the Spirit and participate in the Spirit's work. Cooperating, participating, pursuing, and producing the Fruit of the Spirit are accomplished by setting our minds on the things of the Spirit:

> *For those who live according to the flesh set their minds on the things of the flesh, but those who live according to the Spirit, the things of the Spirit.* Romans 8:5

> *Set your mind on things above, not on things on the earth.* Colossians 3:2

> *Finally, brethren, whatever things are true, whatever things are noble, whatever things are just, whatever things are pure, whatever things are lovely, whatever things are of good report, if there is any virtue and if there is anything praiseworthy—meditate on these things.* Philippians 4:8

166

There is no mistaking the connection between a mind set on the things of God and knowing God's will in your life. Our minds must be fixed on God to know God's will. This doesn't come naturally, however; it is a discipline that must be reinforced through practice and persistence.

There can be no clearer association found between knowing the will of God and our mindset than what we find in Romans 12:2: *"And do not be conformed to this world, but be transformed by the renewing of your mind, that you may prove what is that good and acceptable and perfect will of God."* Don't miss the radical change that Paul is demanding we must make. We cannot continue as we always have. We must be changed. We must be transformed in the way we think, in what we think, and in how we think. It is the only way that will lead us down the road of understanding God's perfect will for our lives.

The word *transformed* carries with it the idea of a metamorphosis. The first thing that probably comes to mind is the type of life-altering change that takes a caterpillar and metamorphoses him into a butterfly, a change that not only beautifies him, but also frees him to rise to new heights. What once was unimaginable, as a caterpillar, has become possible through the metamorphosis. As Paul wrote, *"Therefore, if anyone is in Christ, he is a new creation; old things have passed away; behold, all things have become new"* (2 Corinthians 5:17).

This is a change that makes us beautiful, a change that frees us to rise to new heights. Heights that were once inconceivable apart from Christ now have become possible because the old things have passed, all things have become new in Christ, and all things have become possible. With a new mind, a transformed mind, a mind that is fixed upon the things of God and no longer the things of the world, we are now able to understand and know what the perfect will of God is for our lives. I love how A.W Tozer gives us a very practical technique for fixing our minds on the things of God. It begins with our approach to the Word of God:

Read it much, read it often, brood over it, think over it, meditate over it—meditate on the Word of God day and night. When you wake at night, think of a verse. When you get up in the morning, no matter how you feel, think of a verse and make the Word of God everything.

Because the Holy Ghost wrote the Word, and if you will make a lot of the Word, He will make a lot of you. For it is through the Word that God reveals Himself. This is not a dead book between covers; it is a living, vibrant book. God wrote it and it is still alive . . . God is in this book. The Holy Ghost is in this book. And if you want to find Him, go into the book.[9]

It takes commitment to seek God day after day, when it's convenient and when it is inconvenient, when it is easy and when it is difficult, when you feel like it and when you don't. Having a mind fixed on God and the things of God is essential if we desire to know what His will is for our lives.

If this hasn't been your approach to God, then the good news is that it is never too late to renew your mind and to set it on the things above. The result of setting your mind on the things of God and allowing the Spirit to work in and through your life will be a great harvest for the Kingdom of God. What you spend your time thinking about will show itself in what you spend your time doing.

How much time do you spend thinking about the things of God? How much time do you spend doing the things of God? Noble thoughts lead to noble actions. Virtuous thoughts lead to virtuous actions. Christ-like thoughts lead to Christ-like actions. If you spend more time thinking about worldly things, then make the change today and begin to renew your mind by seeking Him and setting your mind on Him. Then watch the fruit begin to flow from your life in abundance. As we walk in the Spirit and are led by the Spirit, we will produce the Fruit of the Spirit.

The Perfect Gift

I don't know of anyone who doesn't like to receive a present. There is something exciting about tearing into the wrapping paper, with every pull of the paper bringing you that much closer to unveiling the gift inside. It is especially exciting when the present is from someone who knows you very well, because they know what you have and don't have. They know what you like and what you don't like. Therefore, they can pick out the perfect gift for you.

Another aspect to discovering God's will for your life involves unwrapping the gifts the Holy Spirit has given to every believer in Jesus Christ. There is no greater gift-giver than God, because He is the one who knows you perfectly and personally. He has created you, and the Bible tells us that He has given every member in the Body of Christ a gift: " . . . *each one has his own gift from God . . .*" (1 Corinthians 7:7) and " . . . *each one has received a gift . . .*" (1 Peter 4:10).

Not knowing your spiritual gift is like leaving the most valuable present ever given to you unopened. Don't waste such a valuable gift, open it up and discover all God has planned for you to accomplish through that special gift.

Before you can adequately determine what gift or gifts you possess, you must first know what the Gifts of the Spirit are. The Bible clearly lists out twenty special spiritual gifts of the Holy Spirit for the equipping of the saints for the work of the ministry. The gifts of the Holy Spirit can be found in three passages: Romans 12, 1 Corinthians 12, and Ephesians 4. Let me briefly go over them in the order they appear, eliminating any repetition, thereby giving you a basic understanding of the gifts so you may be better prepared to determine which gift or gifts God has given to you.

Romans 12

1. *Prophecy*: speaking for God and giving His message.

2. *Ministry/serving:* seeing tasks that need to be done and using the needed resources to accomplish them.

3. *Teaching*: the ability to take the Word of God and convey it to God's people in such a way that it can be clearly understood and applied.

4. *Exhorting/encouraging:* to come alongside to comfort and challenge someone to live God's best.

5. *Giving:* the ability to give financially to the work of the ministry with an attitude of cheerfulness and generosity.

6. *Leadership:* the ability to motivate and work through others to accomplish God-given goals.

7. *Mercy:* compassion for those who are in need or suffering, and the ability to help bring them comfort.

1 Corinthians 12

8. *Word of wisdom*: the ability to apply biblical truth, often in a specific situation.

9. *Word of knowledge:* the ability to receive God-given facts (insight) about a situation.

10. *Faith:* exceptional ability to believe and trust God's ability to work.

11. *Healing:* the gift in which God is able to heal the sick (mentally, physically, and emotionally) through you.

12. *Miracles:* God's working through you to accomplish something supernatural.

13. *Discernment:* the ability to make a distinction as to whether someone or something is speaking truth or error and whether it is of God.

14. *Tongues:* the ability to speak in a previously unknown language for the purpose of edification.

15. *Interpretation:* the ability to interpret tongues.

16. *Apostle:* a person who is sent out as messenger of the gospel to new areas.

17. *Helps:* supporting others and freeing them up for other ministry.

18. *Administration:* the ability to plan, guide, and organize in order to accomplish tasks.

Ephesians 4

19. *Evangelism:* the ability and desire to communicate the gospel message.

20. *Shepherd/pastor:* the ability to care for the spiritual needs of God's people.

Gifts versus talents

One important distinction that should be made here is that gifts are different from talents. For example, being a good musician is not a spiritual gift; it is a talent that is also given by God, but it is separate from a spiritual gift.

Or, you may like working with your hands, which is also a talent, and it may be related to your spiritual gift. It may even help you to determine what your spiritual gift is. But talents and gifts are distinctly different, and we must not confuse the two. In working with your hands, for example, you might find that you have the gift of helps or the gift of serving. Both are often very hands-on aspects of ministry, and through using your talent, you may discover what your spiritual gift is.

Here is one final example to help make the distinction: singing is not a spiritual gift, but if people are blessed by your use of that talent, you may find that you have the gift of encouragement, and through the use of that talent, you are also exercising your spiritual gift. Worship leaders often will fall into this category, as they use their talent of music and singing to encourage and exhort the Body of Christ.

The bottom line is that it is good to know what your talents are, but it is even more important to know your spiritual gifting so you can do everything possible to ensure you are living and serving God according to His perfect will for your life. We honor God by knowing and using the gifts He has given the Body of Christ to use in blessing the Body of Christ. So don't leave your gift unopened. If we want to see God accomplish the most in and through our lives, then we need to know the spiritual gift(s) He has given to each of us. This way, we can, as Oswald Chambers put it, give our "utmost for His highest."

Discovering Your Spiritual Gifts

So how does someone find out what his or her spiritual gifts are? Let me start by saying it is not through one of those online spiritual gift tests. Although they may be fun and interesting, there are no shortcuts in the process. Nor is there a machine where you can put in a quarter, pull a lever, and expect your spiritual gift to come tumbling out. It takes time and effort to determine your spiritual gifts. It is not a matter of picking and choosing, either. It isn't like some sort of spiritual buffet where you say, "Oh, that gift looks good! I'll take some teaching with a side of helps—and a scoop of prophecy."

This is the sort of misguided desire that got the Corinthians into trouble (see 1 Corinthians 12). Gifts are given by the Holy Spirit in accordance with God's will for your life, not according to your desire for a particular gift. Where the Corinthians got into trouble, and where we can get into trouble, is when we begin to desire gifts God has given to others. Our greatest desire in using our spiritual gifts should be to use the ones God has given us for His glory. The best spiritual gift is the gift God has given to you.

The Apostle Paul posed this question: *"Are all apostles? Are all prophets? Are all teachers? Are all workers of miracles? Do all have gifts of healings? Do all speak with tongues? Do all interpret?"* (1Corintians 12:29-30). The obvious answer is no. Each one of us has different gifts, differing according to the grace of God, all working together for the edification and exhortation of the Body of Christ, all done for the glory of God. We need to not only know what our gifts are, but we must also be content with what God has given us and how He has called us to serve Him with those gifts for the benefit of His Kingdom. John MacArthur says it well:

> *Every believer receives the exact gift and resources best suited to fulfill his role in the body of Christ. . . . Every person has his own special but limited set of capabilities. Trying to operate outside those capabilities produces frustration, discouragement, guilt feelings, mediocrity, and ultimate defeat. We fulfill our calling when we function according to God's sovereign design for us.*[10]

Therefore, the place to start in determining the gifts God has given to you is through prayer. Purposeful prayer in this area starts by seeking and asking God to reveal the spiritual gifts He has given to you. Jesus said, "So I say to you, ask, and it will be given to you; seek, and you will find; knock, and it will be opened to you. For everyone who asks receives, and he who seeks finds, and to him who knocks it will be opened" (Luke 11:9-10).

God has given you a gift (or gifts), and part of His will for you is to know what that gift is so you can use it all for the glory of God. So simply start by asking Him to show you, to give you the wisdom to know, and the boldness to go and serve.

Next, do a little self-examination as you prayerfully look over the list of spiritual gifts. Ask yourself, *What do I enjoy doing?* Write down the gifts that seem to stand out to you, the ones you enjoy doing, the ones that seem to come naturally to you. It stands to reason that if God gives you the gift, He also will give you the ability to use the gift, and he will give you the desire to do so.

For example, if you constantly worry about money, and it is a constant source of anxiety, simple observation says it is likely the gift of giving isn't one of your gifts. On the other hand, if giving to others is something that you love to do, and you find that whether you have a little money or a lot, it just brings you great joy to give to the work of the ministry or to someone in need, then it stands to reason that giving may be one of your spiritual gifts.

All this to say that as you examine your life, you should find joy and ability associated with the gifts God has given to you. You also should note there is often a little trial and error associated with this self-discovery of your spiritual gifts. As you serve in various ministry opportunities, you will notice not only those things you enjoy doing, but also those things you are able to do, those things you are able to do very well, and those things you are not able to do. You should take special notice of the thing you are able to do well and brings you the most joy, as this may be your primary gift. Even though you may have more than one gift, there should be one gift that stands out as the primary gift, which is that thing you do the best.

Next, seek confirmation. Stop, look, and listen to what trusted believers you know have to say about what they see through your service to the Lord. Listen to those believers whom you consider to be mature and wise. It may be a pastor, an elder, a spiritual mentor, a leader of a ministry, or just a close friend who has a proven walk with the Lord. Ask their input on what they have observed in your Christian life. Others should be able to see your spiritual gift and help provide you with some confirmation to support your gifting.

For example, if you think you have a certain gift, do those whom you look to for advice share the same opinion? If you feel you have the gift of teaching, are people listening to you? Are others being blessed by what you teach? I am not talking about reaching perfection, although you always should be growing in the use of your gifts, but you should be able to see that others are being blessed and also recognize the gift of teaching in you. If no one thinks you are a teacher, then maybe, just maybe, it isn't your spiritual gift.

Lastly, availability is so important in the process of determining your spiritual gift. Make yourself available to God to be used by God, and wait and see what opportunities God brings your way. It was stated earlier that God doesn't care so much about your *ability* as He does your *availability*. I believe this is often the case as we seek to serve God. God is seeking willing vessels. The Bible tells us He often uses the foolish things of this world to confound the wise. Why? Because it isn't our ability that gets the spiritual job done; it's His. As you make yourself available to God, He will give you the wisdom you need to determine your gifts so you can live and serve in the center of His will for your life.

Once you have spent time discovering your gift, have received the confirmation you need, and you see there is fruit coming from the use of your gift, then use your gift or gifts to the fullest extent possible.

We are reminded in 1 Peter 4:10:

As each one has received a gift, minister it to one another, as good stewards of the manifold grace of God.

And let's heed the warning given by the Apostle Paul to Timothy:

Do not neglect the gift that is in you . . . 1 Timothy 4:14

Paul also had this to say about spiritual gifts:

Having then gifts differing according to the grace that is given to us, let us use them . . . Romans 12:6

For we are His workmanship, created in Christ Jesus for good works, which God prepared beforehand that we should walk in them. Ephesians 2:10

God has prepared a work for us to do and He has given us all the necessary gifts to accomplish that work.

Spirit-led

Discovering God's will and following His will for our lives cannot be done apart from the help of the Holy Spirit. He has given us His Spirit, so we are Spirit-filled, but we must also be Spirit-led so we can live in the Spirit and walk in the Spirit.

The Holy Spirit does not lead us by our emotions, our feelings, or our own wisdom. We must remember that emotions and feelings are matters of the heart. As the prophet Jeremiah so clearly teaches us, *"The heart is deceitful above all things, and desperately wicked . . ."* (Jeremiah 17:9).

Now, emotions are not bad; God gave them to us. Therefore, at the very base level, they have a purpose. However, we can get into trouble when we are led by our emotions, allowing them to rule over us, which often will lead us away from God. Our emotions are not to be our guide in life. They are not to be out in front. This is a recipe for disaster. Proverbs 3:5 says, *"Trust in the*

Lord with all your heart, and lean not on your own understanding . . ." Notice something very important here. This verse does *not* tell us to trust in our heart or to lean on our own understanding. As Christians, we are to place our trust in *the Lord.*

If we trust in our heart, it will lead us astray—not to mention there would be an absence of absolute authority. How so? Without some absolute authority, everyone would do as he or she pleased, each following the leading of the heart, each person using the heart as his or her personal authority.

Unfortunately, this is what we largely see in the world today. We have a world that says and believes the adage, "Listen to your heart," when God says, "Listen to Me." To be a Christian and to follow your heart means that you are leaning on your own understanding, and to act in this manner is to immediately step away from the leading of the Holy Spirit. I have met many Christians who are simply doing what they want to do. They try to justify their actions with the readied response, "the Spirit is leading me," as if that is some sort of spiritual trump card they can play to end all further discussion on the subject.

As believers, God tells us that we are to be yielded to His Spirit's leading, and we need to allow God to search our hearts, try us, and test us so that we may know whether there is any selfish desire in us. This will enable us to see clearly if we are being led by His Spirit or by our own desires. When it comes to following God, listening to your heart, or leaning on your own understanding, is the worst possible course of action. Proverbs 28:26 warns, *"He who trusts in his own heart is a fool. . . ."* We are not to trust in our hearts or in our limited understanding. We are called to be more purposeful in following God than merely doing what feels right.

Our hearts, our wisdom, and our understanding are limited, but God's is limitless. Our hearts, knowledge, and understanding change, waver, falter, flutter, and will generally mislead us. God, on the other hand, is immovable, unshakable, unchangeable, all-knowing, and all-powerful. Therefore, we are to place our trust in the one and only source of truth: God, who alone is wise.

God is always seeking to conform us into the image of Christ, and two good questions to ask yourself in determining whether the Spirit is leading you to do something are: *Does this work to conform me into the image of Christ? Is this working to conform others into the image of Christ?*

When you place Christ at the center of your discernment process, you are much more likely to see His will rather than your own.

Now What?

How many times have you asked yourself the question, "Now what?"

For me, there have been many different times and many different reasons I have asked that question. I remember one time in particular. I was in college, and I had just spent four years studying, taking tests, writing papers, acquiring information upon information, and it was now graduation time. That question hit me like a ton of bricks: "Now what?"

There comes a time in all our lives called the moment of truth. It's a time when the student now puts his or her education into practice, a time when an athlete stops training and runs the race, and a time when the Christian lives what he or she believes and begins obeying the Word of God rather than just hearing it.

It is important to take time throughout your walk with Christ to discover God's general will and His specific will for your life, because God wants to bless you. The Christian life is a lifelong journey in which God has a plan for your life. He wants to use you, He has given you gifts He wants you to exercise, and everything about His will for your life and the using of those gifts is good. So we need to understand this aspect of our relationship with God. As Ephesians 5:17 says, *"Therefore do not be unwise, but understand what the will of the Lord is."*

Even when we are in the midst of trials, suffering, persecutions, or one of the many difficulties we may face along life's journey, we must always remember what God has said: *"For I know the thoughts that I think toward you, says the Lord, thoughts of peace and not of evil, to give you a future and a hope"* (Jeremiah 29:11). Psalm 56:8 says God even saves our tears.

God wastes nothing. He uses everything in our lives. God even uses the difficulties to accomplish His plans and purposes, as we have already seen in the lives of both Moses and Joseph. When we are trying to determine God's will in times of difficulty, suffering, or trials, we need to pray and ask the Lord to give us both wisdom and understanding as to how He wants to use these circumstances for His highest glory and His holiest will—for our lives or in the lives of others. As David prayed, *"Teach me to do Your will, for You are my God . . ."* (Psalm 143:10).

It is specifically in the midst of trying circumstances and adversity that we need to not give up, but dig deep and seek to apply biblical truths personally, live them practically, and practice them habitually. We need to take what we have learned and are learning from the Word of God and *just do it*. In the midst of whatever may be happening, we need to take our eyes off our circumstances and fix them on the Lord.

It is not easy to be a doer of the Word when you are in the midst of a storm, but however difficult it may be, we are reminded and challenged in James 1:22: *"But be doers of the word, and not hearers only, deceiving yourselves."*

We do not want to become like the religious leaders in the parable of the Good Samaritan (see Luke 10) who knew a lot about God, but their knowledge did nothing to transform their lives. As a result, they missed the opportunity to be used to bless someone else. These men held a lot of head knowledge, but had not applied it to become heart understanding. They *knew about* God, but they didn't *live for* God.

Living the Christian life, I believe, is being able to put into practice what we already know to be true from God's Word, making it a part of our everyday lives. If we make it our aim to be living what we know and learn, then we will be well on our way to living God's best for our lives. Don't just take my word for it. Take a final lesson from one of the great men of church history, George Mueller, a man who definitely lived out what he learned from God's Word. This is what he wrote about knowing God's will:

I seek to get my heart into such a state that it has no will of its own in a given matter . . . Nine-tenths of the difficulties are overcome when our hearts are ready to do the Lord's will, whatever it may be . . .

Having done this, I do not leave the result to feeling or simple impression. If so, I make myself liable to great delusions.

I seek the will of the Spirit of God through, or in connection with, the Word of God. The Spirit and the Word must be combined. If I look to the Spirit alone without the Word, I lay myself open to great delusions also. If the Holy Ghost guides us at all, He will do it according to the Scriptures and never contrary to them.

Next, I take into account providential circumstances. These often plainly indicate God's Will in connection with His Word and Spirit.

I ask God in prayer to reveal His will to me . . .

Thus, through prayer to God, the study of the Word, and reflection, I come to a deliberate judgment according to the best of my ability and knowledge, and if my mind is thus at peace, and continues so after two or three more petitions, I proceed accordingly. In trivial matters, and in transactions involving most important issues, I have found this method always effective.[11]

My prayer for every believer is the same prayer the Apostle Paul prayed for the believers in Colossae:

"For this reason we also, since the day we heard it, do not cease to pray for you, and to ask that you may be filled with the knowledge of His will in all wisdom and spiritual understanding; that you may walk worthy of the Lord, fully pleasing Him, being fruitful in every good work and increasing in the knowledge of God."
Colossians 1:9-10

Paul added to this heartfelt prayer in Ephesians 3:16-19, and so will I. Now may God

. . . grant you, according to the riches of His glory, to be strengthened with might through His Spirit in the inner man, that Christ may dwell in your hearts through faith; that you, being rooted and grounded in love, may be able to comprehend with all the saints what is the width and length and depth and height—to know the love of Christ which passes knowledge; that you may be filled with all the fullness of God.

From my heart to yours, may you always seek to live God's will, God's way, in God's time, for God's glory.

Final Thoughts

Following God is a lifelong commitment. It isn't something you decide to do one day and not the next. It requires faithfulness and obedience, discipline and repetition. It isn't about tradition or religion, but it is a personal relationship. As a relationship, it requires time, communication, and sacrifice.

There is no magical formula for following God. You can't say, "Well, if I do all that Joseph did, I'll be blessed," and decide to throw yourself into a pit, sell yourself as a slave, put yourself in prison, and then say, "Okay, God, bless me like Joseph." It doesn't work that way. God has an individual plan for each individual person. But what we can do is take the godly qualities we see from Joseph's life and apply them to our lives. We can trust God as Joseph trusted God, and in turn, we can expect God to do great things in and through us.

Moses reminds me constantly of the importance of obedience. Where man's strength is small, God's strength is complete and perfect. Where man's wisdom is limited, God's wisdom is total and absolute. He knows the beginning from the end, and if we wait upon God to guide us, if we follow His lead instead of trying to lead Him, then we will see miraculous things happen. The waters of trouble will part, we will see Him lead us as clearly as the children of Israel saw a cloud during the day and fire at night, and He will feed us in ways that far surpass the miraculous manna from Heaven.

God's Holy Spirit has been given to us to be our Helper. He is our internal God Positioning System. He helps us make sense of truth and discern lies. He empowers us to do the work to which He has called us. He gives us different gifts so that the Body is balanced. He is our comfort in times of trouble. He teaches, counsels, speaks to our hearts, produces fruit in our lives, seals us until the day of our redemption, brings us into fellowship with God and other believers, brings conviction, and so much more. He is the strongest force, empowering us to live God's will. Let us not quench His work in our lives.

Coming Full Circle
HOW TO
Know God

∽

Knowing God will absolutely, totally, completely, and radically change your life. His plan for your life starts by knowing God's Son, Jesus Christ. The Bible says:

> *For this is good and acceptable in the sight of God our Savior, who desires all men to be saved and to come to the knowledge of the truth. For there is one God and one Mediator between God and men, the Man Christ Jesus, who gave Himself a ransom for all . . . 1 Timothy 2:3-6*

God's top priority for you and for me is faith in Jesus. Jesus is the starting point in the long walk of faith. Jesus is the only way to secure a future in Heaven with God, the Father. This is not about religion. Religion brings the traditions of men, rules and regulations, but a relationship—a personal, life-changing and intimate relationship with God—brings freedom and love.

It's not about church; it's about Christ. It's not about what you can *do* for God; it is about what God has already *done* for you.

But in order to begin a relationship with God in which you truly will be free, there are four things that need to happen.

Listen to God

To know what God says about salvation, we must look at the only source for spiritual truth, the only place where thinking can become knowing: the Bible. The Bible is God's love letter, written to mankind, written in His very own blood. He doesn't just give us rules and regulations; He gives us the secrets to joy and peace, to blessing and happiness, to everlasting life and holy living. We rob ourselves of these and so much more if we fail to take the time and listen to what He has said by reading His Holy and perfect Word.

Every person needs to know what God has said about us, and the best place to begin is in the Book of Romans.

As it is written:

There is none righteous, no, not one. Romans 3:10

For all have sinned and fall short of the glory of God. Romans 3:23 [emphasis added]

We are definitely not off to a great start, are we? Simply put, we have a problem. God has given this problem a name. (No, it is not your neighbor, your spouse, or your boss.) The problem's name is sin. You may be thinking, *Sin? That sounds a little harsh, don't you think? I mean, I'm not a bad person. I've never killed anyone or anything.*

All that may be true. You may be a good person by the world's standards, but if you want to spend eternity with God, then it is His standard you need to be concerned about.

What is sin then, and why does God say it is a problem? The Bible tells us the Law—and we will confine our consideration of the Law to the Ten Commandments for now—was given to us so that we might know what sin is. We read in Romans 7:7, *"What shall we say then? Is the law sin? Certainly not! On the contrary, I would not have known sin except through the law. For I would not have known covetousness unless the law had said, 'You shall not covet.'"*

The Law in the Old Testament—or for our purposes, the Ten Commandments found in Exodus 20—gives us the standard by which God looks at man and how God sees you and me. We must understand that we all have broken God's Law. The above passage from Romans 7 tells us that as we break that Law, God calls it sin, and every person who has ever lived has broken God's law. All are guilty—no exceptions, no excuses. There is *one* exception. There is someone who is perfect and free from sin, and His name is Jesus. Jesus is God, and as God, He cannot sin. But the rest of us have all thought, said, or done something at one time or another to break God's Law.

In the New Testament, Matthew 5-7 records how Jesus clarifies and defines sin. In these chapters, Jesus explains that the thoughts and desires within our hearts and minds also count as sin. Sin isn't just about an action or outward expression. The commission of sin actually begins at the moment it becomes a thought. Jesus explained in the Book of Matthew that if you hate someone in your heart, then you are guilty of murder (see Matthew 5:21-22). If you lust after another person in your heart, then you are guilty of adultery (see Matthew 5:27-28), and so on. This is sin at its basic form, and it starts in our thoughts, moves to our heart, and then becomes our actions. And this is what God tells us our problem is.

Look At Yourself

After we listen to what God says about our spiritual condition, we can begin to see and understand that we all have a problem called sin. So the next thing we need to do is to take a look at ourselves. Just as an X-ray gives us a look at the inside of the physical person, God's Word gives us an inside look into the spiritual person.

Like an X-ray held up to the light, the first thing we notice on our spiritual film is a dark spot, and it is rooted deep within our heart. If we take an open and honest look at ourselves next to the light of God's Word, it is both unmistakable and undeniable that we have a heart problem.

We have considered briefly the problem God identifies as sin. Now let's take a similar look at how sin affects each one of us. When we boil sin down to its simplest form, sin is selfishness. It is placing our own will, thoughts, desires, wants, cares, and concerns first. When we place anything before God, this is sin at its simplest form. The first of the Ten Commandments says, *"You shall have no other gods before Me"* (Exodus 20:3). The nature of sin always says, "Me first!" When people choose to sin, they are, in that moment of decision, saying, choosing, and doing as they desire, because they have given priority to their wants and will. No matter how a person may justify it, rationalize it, or try to explain it away, the fact of the matter doesn't change: it is still sin. Self before God is always sin.

The problem we have is we don't like to admit that we are sinners in need of a Savior, especially when we live in a world that is shouting, "If it feels good, do it," or "If it makes you happy, it can't be wrong"—along with a host of other self-serving ideologies. The bottom line is we want to do what we want to do, when we want to do it, and we don't want anyone telling us we can't.

When we understand what sin is and then acknowledge that we have sinned, it means we recognize God's way is perfect, and our way is imperfect. We admit we make mistakes and at the core of our hearts, we are all sinners. This may be an offensive message to many. We don't like to hear that we are not good. We don't like it when people tell us we are wrong. We want to believe that deep down inside we are all good, that we are right, and that we know best. Proverbs 16:2 says, *"All the ways of a man are pure in his own eyes, but the Lord weighs the spirits."* And according to Proverbs 21:2, *"Every way of a man is right in his own eyes, but the Lord weighs the hearts."* The problem with thinking we are right is since there are billions of people in the world, it means there are billions of perspectives—and they all can't be right. That is why one standard is needed, and that standard is God's Word.

Standing in contrast to the world's view is God's view, a view that says we are to be Christ-serving, not self-serving, and Christ-centered, not self-centered. It is a belief that offers hope for the sinner and a truth that says there is a cure for that dark spot on our spiritual X-ray.

Look At the Cross

God's wants all of us to have a relationship with Him. He wants all of us to experience the joy and peace in this life that comes as we begin taking care of that dark spot of sin. Even though we are sinners, God still loves us, and it was out of His love for us that He was motivated to provide a cure for the problem of sin. So where do we find this cure? The Cross is where we must look:

> *For God so loved the world that He gave His only begotten Son, that whoever believes in Him should not perish but have everlasting life. For God did not send His Son into the world to condemn the world, but that the world through Him might be saved.* John 3:16-17

For it pleased the Father that in Him all the fullness should dwell, and by Him to reconcile all things to Himself, by Him, whether things on earth or things in heaven, having made peace through the blood of His cross. Colossians 1:19-20

The Cross is the place where God provided both a sacrifice for sin and an opportunity for us to have a right relationship with God. Sin had to be judged, and Jesus was the one willing to pay the penalty we deserved. And because He was sinless, He was the only sacrifice God would accept on our behalf for our sins:

For if when we were enemies we were reconciled to God through the death of His Son, much more, having been reconciled, we shall be saved by His life. Romans 5:10

Jesus said to him, "I am the way, the truth, and the life. No one comes to the Father except through Me." John 14:6

Simply put, Jesus took our place, paid the price, and God was satisfied. In His substitutionary death, Jesus took our guilt upon himself and paid the penalty for it. What God now wants from us is for us to enter into a relationship with Him, through faith in the finished work of Jesus Christ on the Cross. To do that, we must acknowledge our sinful state and that His death paid our debt in full. It is here that forgiveness is now granted to all who will believe.

Speak to God

The fourth and final step involves taking a moment to speak to God in prayer. Prayer is simply having a conversation with God. All too often, prayer is viewed as some high and lofty speech that only a trained scholar in theology should even attempt. That is not the case, however.

Prayer is an open line of communication with God that is available to us 24/7. Prayer can be short, or it can be long. You can pray for two minutes or two hours, you can pray in your car or on your knees. It doesn't matter the amount of time or the physical position you take; the only aspect of prayer that matters is that you speak to God from your heart.

Prayer is not the time or place to try and impress God with your eloquence or persuasive speech, because He looks at the heart. The sincerity that flows from a transparent and honest heart before God is what He responds to. Our first prayer, or conversation with God, should begin with confession. Romans 10:9-10 tells us, *"If you* confess *with your mouth the Lord Jesus and believe in your heart that God has raised Him from the dead, you will be saved. For with the heart one believes unto righteousness, and with the mouth* confession *is made unto salvation"* (emphasis added).

This Scripture passage summarizes basic belief in Jesus. It tells us that Jesus is Lord, which means He is God, and that as God, He is to be the one in charge of our lives. It also tells us that Jesus died for our sins and God raised Him from the dead, conquering death through His Resurrection and bringing eternal life to all who believe. This is to be at the core of our confession and our first prayer to God.

Below is a simple example of what your prayer might sound like. If this isn't a step of faith you have taken in your life, if this confession hasn't been made, even if you go to church or read your Bible, then this would be a good time to take that step. Remember, this is between you and God. As long as you mean this prayer from your heart, God will hear your prayer, heal your broken relationship with Him, and help you walk in newness of life. Simply pray:

Lord, I come to you today, and I ask you to forgive me of all my sins. I believe Jesus is the Son of God and that He died on the Cross for my sins so I may be forgiven. I believe God raised Him from the dead, and by placing my faith in Jesus, I can have eternal life. I ask you, God, to come into my life today and fill me with your Holy Spirit. Help me to live a life that is pleasing to you. I ask all this in the name of my Savior, Jesus Christ. Amen.

It is amazing and true that right now, this very second, there is a party going on in Heaven if this was your prayer today! And if you have just prayed this prayer, there are a few promises I would like to share with you—promises and blessings, gifts from God written in the Bible that are now yours to possess and that you can apply to your life immediately:

For whoever calls on the name of the Lord shall be saved. Romans 10:13

Likewise, I say to you, there is joy in the presence of the angels of God over one sinner who repents. Luke 15:10

Therefore, having been justified by faith, we have peace with God through our Lord Jesus Christ. Romans 5:1

"For I know the thoughts that I think toward you," says the Lord, *"thoughts of peace and not of evil, to give you a future and a hope."* Jeremiah 29:11

How wonderful to begin a relationship with God, to enter into a new season of blessing and peace with God. The Bible is full of promises for the believer, and you will have a lifetime of joy as you discover them. You will spend your life discovering who God is, finding out who you are in Him, learning who you were created to be in Christ, and walking in the great things God wants to do through your life.

Nothing could be more exciting and more meaningful than to walk with God, to find your purpose in life, and to know the very one who created you.

END NOTES

1. C. H. Spurgeon, *The Metropolitan Tabernacle Pulpit: Sermons Preached and Revised by C.H. Spurgeon during the Year 1877*, vol. 23 (London: Passmore & Alabaster, Steam Printers, 1878), 32.

2. Martin Luther King, Jr., "I Have a Dream" speech text, *Martin Luther King Online,* http://www.mlkonline. net/dream.html.

3. M.G. Easton, *Easton's Bible Dictionary* (Oak Harbor, WA: Logos Research Systems, Inc., 1996, 1897).

4. *Merriam Webster's Collegiate Dictionary,* 11th ed., s.v. "envy" (Springfield, Mass.: Merriam-Webster, Inc., 2003), 418.

5. R. Kent Hughes, *Genesis: Beginning and Blessing* (Wheaton, Ill.: Crossway Books, 2004), 471.

6. Dr. I. M. Haldeman, as quoted by Arthur W. Pink, *Gleanings in Exodus* (Chicago: Moody Press, 1981), 16.

7. Charles Henry Mackintosh, as quoted by Arthur W. Pink, *Gleanings in Exodus* (Chicago: Moody Press, 1981), 23.

8. John Calvin, *Institutes of the Christian Religion*, ed. John T. McNeill, trans. Ford Lewis Battles (Philadelphia: Westminster, 1960), 20–21.

9. A. W. Tozer, *Tozer: Mystery of the Holy Spirit* (Alachua, Fla.: Bridge-Logos, 2007), 119.

10. John MacArthur, *The MacArthur New Testament Commentary: Romans 9-16* (Chicago: Moody Publishers, 1994), 161.

11. George Müller, *Answers to Prayer* (Middlesex, UK: The Echo Library, 2008), 4.